THE CROSS AND THE KREMLIN

MARK A. FINLEY

HART RESEARCH CENTER
FALLBROOK, CALIFORNIA

Edited by Ken McFarland
Cover design by Ed Guthero
Cover illustration by Nathan Greene
Photos by Ernestine Finley and
Brook and Gloria Benzinger

Printed in the United States of America
by Pacific Press Specialty Printing

ISBN: 1-878046-12-8

Contents

Also Available From Hart Research Center

In addition to this book and the accompanying cassette album, other outreach resources are available from Hart Research Center:

For information, write:
Hart Research Center
P.O. Box 2377
Fallbrook, CA 92088

Or call:
(619) 723-8082 [pricing and other information]
(800) 487-4278 [orders *only*, please!]

FOREWORD

Which New Testament book—other than one of the Gospels—is the most inspiring and stimulating? Isn't it the Acts of the Apostles? Healing episodes, traumatic beatings and imprisonments, the first church council, Paul's shipwreck, the stoning of Stephen, a king dying from a terrific case of worms—all make this book come alive with excitement!

One facet of this inspiring record deals with astonishing statistical reports. It begins with 3,000 being brought to Christ, then 5,000, then "a considerable number," and finally, multitudes. (See Acts 2:41; 4:4; 11:24, NASB.)

In the autumn of 1990, my wife, Marie, and I had an experience similar to that revealed in the Book of Acts. We held several short meetings, including one in Moscow. Advertising was minimal, and thousands attended and kept attending. Literally hundreds stood in the aisles, jammed the doorways, and begged for more Bibles.

As a result of our experience, in January, 1991, the greatest evangelistic program our church has ever launched took place in the former U.S.S.R. Private donations sent to our Adventist world headquarters poured in. Hundreds of thousands of Bibles were printed and purchased. Scores of thousands of people enrolled in the twenty-four-lesson Bible course. New churches were established. In 1991 our membership in the former Soviet Union increased by a phenomenal thirty percent, making it the fastest growing Division in our world church.

What you are about to read is the remarkable, yes, and miraculous story of a series of meetings sponsored by the General Conference of the worldwide Seventh-day Adventist Church in the very seat of Communism—the Kremlin Congressional Hall—where the atheistic Communists held their large party conventions. This is the fulfillment of a dream I have had since our first visit to this sealed country in 1984.

It is quite impossible for any reader to imagine what it means to an entire nation of over 280 million to experience religious and political freedom for the first time in over one thousand years. Before the Bolshevik revolution in 1917, the masses were controlled by a church-state relationship dominated by the Czars and the Russian Orthodox Church. Today these masses have the opportunity of listening freely to the gospel preached in public places.

We know not what the future holds, but we are determined to preach Christ and Him crucified as long as the doors remain open. By the end of 1992, we will have held over seventy-five major gospel crusades in the former Soviet Union, resulting in the doubling of our church membership there.

Please praise God as you read the stories in this book, which is nothing less than a repetition of the Book of Acts, dressed in twentieth-century garb.

J.R. Spangler
Consultant for Evangelism for the
Seventh-day Adventist Euro-Asia Division
(formerly the U.S.S.R.)

About the Author

Mark A. Finley is the Speaker-elect of It Is Written—an international telecast of the Seventh-day Adventist Church based in Thousand Oaks, California. As this book is published, he is scheduled to become the Speaker-Director for the widely aired program in September of 1992.

Following graduation from Atlantic Union College in 1967, he began his ministry in the Seventh-day Adventist Church as a pastor in the Southern New England Conference, and later, the Georgia-Cumberland Conference.

Beginning in 1974, Mark served five years as Ministerial Secretary and Conference Evangelist in the New England Conference. Between 1979 and 1985, he founded and served as the Director of the North American Division Evangelism Institute, based in Illinois.

In 1985, Mark received a Master of Arts in Pastoral Ministry from Andrews University in Berrien Springs, Michigan. That same year, he became the Ministerial Secretary of the Trans-European Division—a position he filled until September of 1990.

For nearly a year, he served as Vice President for Evangelism in the Michigan Conference, until his selection as Speaker-elect for It Is Written.

Pastor Finley has conducted over forty-five major evangelistic campaigns in major world cities on several continents, resulting to date in thousands of decisions for Christ. He has conducted Field Schools of Evangelism for the Andrews University Theological Seminary, both in North America and in Eur- ope. In frequent demand as a speaker at camp meetings and pastor's meetings, Mark is also a prolific writer, having auth-ored at least eight books and written scores of magazine articles.

In addition, he has produced sixteen video presentations on varied aspects of personal and public evangelism, and has developed and presented a variety of seminars on topics varying from prophecy to managing stress.

Mark's family includes his wife, Ernestine—an Associate in Outreach at It Is Written, and three children: Debbie—a physical therapy student at Andrews University; Rebecca—a high school senior at Andrews Academy; and Mark, Jr.—currently in the seventh grade at Ruth Murdoch Elementary School near Andrews University.

PREFACE

For the last ten years, I've had the privilege of conducting large, city-wide public evangelistic meetings. Thousands have attended. In cities such as London, Copenhagen, Stockholm, Helsinki, Belgrade, Budapest, Chicago, and Gdansk, I have experienced the miraculous moving of the Holy Spirit. Hearts have been touched and lives changed as God's grace has brought new life to multitudes.

The gospel is not a lifeless theory. Christ is not merely an ideal to follow. He is alive—and His life-changing power is real!

The Cross and the Kremlin is the dramatic story of God's working in the very heart of the former Soviet Union. Moscow—its capital—was for decades the symbol of godless atheism. The Kremlin—the seat of the Communist government—epitomized antagonism toward God. And the Kremlin Congress Hall perhaps best represented the ideals of the Communist party.

Recently in that Hall, thousands attended my series of Christ-centered presentations entitled "The Bible Way to

New Life." This series was indeed one of the most significant breakthroughs in the history of modern Christianity.

The hand of God is at work in the former Soviet Union. A despotic regime has been swept aside. The Communist government has collapsed. And God has miraculously opened a door for the proclamation of the gospel.

In *The Cross and the Kremlin*, you will read the dramatic account of God's miraculous intervention in the midst of a political storm. You will thrill at how our precious Lord preserved His Word throughout seventy years of godless atheism. You will be inspired as you hear stories of Russian military officers, scientists, government employees, teachers, physicians—and scores of others from a Communist background—who have accepted Jesus Christ. And you will weep with your suffering Russian brothers and sisters who were persecuted during the atheistic Communist years.

This book is lovingly dedicated to two groups of people. First, to those who so willingly sacrificed of their means to provide Bibles, literature, religious pictures, and slides for our Russian pastors—and over twenty tons of food for the new believers. What a blessing you "partners" are! Without your dedicated commitment and financial support, aggressive evangelistic advance in the former Soviet Union would not be possible. Your gifts of love continue to be a major source of blessing.

I also salute the hundreds of young people whose undimmed vision enabled them to seize an opportunity to become actively involved in proclaiming the gospel in Russia.

My own daughter, Rebecca, inspired students at Andrews Academy to donate the funds to purchase 1,200 Bibles. We certainly thank God for these dedicated young people. My wife, Ernestine, coordinated an effort to purchase and ship twenty tons of food to Moscow. The Russian coordinator of food distribution described the response of the hungry Muscovites receiving the food as "incredible!" Scores of people donated funds to make this project a reality. The people of Russia lift their hearts in thanksgiving.

On a more personal note, I want to express deep appreciation to my staff during the Moscow evangelistic meetings. Don and Marge Gray coordinated our Bible school. Dan Benzinger, my associate evangelist, and his wife, Gloria—our crusade vocalists—added their combined talents. Dr. Walter Thompson contributed immensely to the overall program with medical presentations. Al and Ruby Heitzman blended their organizational skills. Scores of times during the meetings, we met in prayer. I praise God for this dedicated, competent staff.

Second, this book is dedicated to those who suffered through the long night of Russian oppression. For seven long decades, they were oppressed, tortured, and often martyred. Yet they have remained faithful even in persecution. Their prayers have ascended to the Lord above. Unprecedented persecution has led to an unprecedented outpouring of the Holy Spirit.

The spiritual revolution taking place today in Russia is in direct response to the prayers of the Russian believers. This book is their story—a story of courage and faithfulness in the face of persecution. And it is His story—the story of God's faithfulness in their persecution—the story of His power in overthrowing Communism.

To Him be the glory and honor and praise—forever!

Mark A. Finley
May 1992

Rebecca Finley carrying some of the 20,000 Bibles distributed to those who attended the evangelistic meetings.

Ernestine Finley with a shipment of Russian Bibles. Committed North American Adventists donated the funds to purchase thousands of Bibles.

Rebecca Finley presenting to a new Russian friend (foreground) one of the 1,200 Bibles donated by Andrews Academy students.

CHAPTER ONE

RUSSIA'S SPIRITUAL REVOLUTION

Tuesday night, August 20, 1991.

The world held its breath, expecting the worst, as tanks rumbled toward the Russian White House. An attack seemed imminent. *Déjà vu.* Was a repeat of the Tienanmen Square massacre in the making?

Bracing for the attack, Boris Yeltsin barricaded himself with his officials in a basement vault behind a steel door twenty inches thick. Meanwhile, at the Kremlin, orders had already been issued for the KGB's Alpha Unit to storm the Russian White House.

Plans called for commandos and paratroopers to clear the way with tanks and bulldozers. The thousands of protestors were to be flushed away with tear gas. Then the building would be stormed from all sides.

But the impossible happened—the commander of the Alpha Unit refused orders. No way was he was going to kill his fellow countrymen. The KGB chief, shocked and furious, had to postpone the assault until another unit could be prepared. But one by one, the commanders of nearly twenty other elite units all refused to attack—even under the threat of a firing squad.

Coup leaders finally managed to assemble an attack force from KGB and army volunteers. Troops fanned out across the streets of Moscow to position themselves for the assault, set for 3 a.m. But despite a city-wide curfew, resistance was strong. Several brave defenders lost their lives.

Increasingly desperate as the night wore on, coup leaders at the Kremlin came to realize that the operation could not be accomplished without massive civilian casualties. As they wavered in uncertainty, morning dawned. Yeltsin emerged from his hideaway, and the 20,000 defenders outside the White House roused themselves awake, hardly daring to believe they had survived the long, dark night.

The coup had failed. One by one, the fleeing conspirators were captured.

What a debt the world owes to those democratic reformers who risked their lives—and to those who actually gave their lives—to defend freedom in Russia!

Leaders of the coup attempt had actually gained control of the Soviet nuclear arsenal. Can you imagine what might have happened if those desperate men had managed to blackmail the west with their political demands and military threats?

What is the real story behind the failed coup? Why didn't it succeed? Is there something more than meets the eye here? Are divine forces holding the winds of disaster in check? Is a supernatural hand holding back the forces of evil?

Maybe the answer may be found in part in the story of a courageous 14-year-old girl perched atop the steel barricade between the oncoming Communist tanks and Boris Yeltsin's Russian White House. Throughout the long night, the gallant teenager had cooked for the Yeltsin forces, ferrying hot soup from her home to the regiment.

In a moment of reprieve as she sat on the barricade, someone handed her a Bible. Quietly she began to read, and the peace of Christ flooded into her soul. In the midst of a political storm, she was at rest. Urged on by the forces of hell, the hard-line Communists' return to power would have closed the door of freedom for this 14 year old to read and study the Bible. The Word of God would have been torn from her hands and thrown into the street. But the sovereign, supreme God of the universe who had so miraculously opened the doors of religious freedom in the Soviet Union was not going to allow them to be slammed shut in a single night. Believers had been tortured, imprisoned, and martyred. They had suffered for years. Their prayers and tears had ascended to the very throne of God.

And now, in response to their faithfulness, God has opened the doors of religious freedom in the former Soviet Union. The Holy Spirit is being poured out. Thousands are seeking God. The Bible is the runaway best seller—the demand far exceeding the supply. Like a mighty, rushing torrent dammed up and held back for years, the pent-up spiritual longings of millions of Russians have been released with the new freedom to discover spiritual truth. Two million Bibles were distributed to believers in 1988 and 1989, with millions more finding their way into eager hands in the early 1990s.

According to western estimates, about half of the former Soviet Union's 280 million people say they have a religious affiliation.

"First the curtain was lifted on the west," says Natasha Shenhenko, a 21-year-old student at Yaroslavl Pedagogical Institute. "Now it's lifted on the church, and people are curious."

A member of the Communist youth league, Shenhenko told *National Geographic Magazine* that "We are trying to replace our belief in Communism with something else." This special "something else" is the message of the Bible—centered in the life of Jesus Christ.

The spiritual revolution taking place in Russia today is one of most significant movements in the world. Before our eyes, totalitarian regimes have been swept aside by the mighty hand of God. An authoritarian government that has oppressed Christian believers for seventy years has collapsed. And the spiritual vacuum in the hearts of over 280 million Russians is being filled by a mighty moving of the Holy Spirit.

Our own It Is Written telecast is making a major spiritual impact on the lives of millions. Carried on thirty-four different stations throughout the former Soviet Union, we have a weekly viewing audience of over a hundred million. Our founder and speaker, George Vandeman, reports that our Russian It Is Written office receives hundreds of letters every week.

God is at work in the former Soviet Union. Tens of thousands are open today to the Word of God. They stand in lines for hours to purchase a Bible. Not long ago in Moscow during the book fair, book sellers representing hundreds of publishers displayed their wares. One Christian publisher offered to distribute free Bibles to anyone who wanted them, as long as they lasted. People lined up for hours to receive the few thousand Bibles available.

It is reported that the line wound past Madalyn Murray O'Hair's booth, which offered literature championing atheism. So many people crowded the line waiting for Bibles that Mrs. O'Hair's representatives became angry and started shouting at them.

But the people shouted back, "We've had enough of atheism. We want the Word of God." Madalyn Murray

O'Hair and her staff could only respond with silence. What a testimony to the barren emptiness of human hearts without God's Word!

Historically, Russia has been a spiritual nation. In A.D. 988, Vladimir the Great was baptized by immersion in the Dnieper River in Kiev, introducing Christianity to Russia. Since that time Christianity has been a part of the country's culture—woven into the very fabric of Russian life. Over the centuries, Russians have always displayed a deep longing to know God and to follow His will.

By the time the Bolshevik revolution took place in October of 1917 and Lenin rose to power, the Orthodox church had become large, formal, and ritualistic—and it obviously lacked in spiritual power. Church leaders united with the Czars. Lavish cathedrals and grandiose palaces were built. The masses lived in abject poverty, while church and state leaders lived in luxury.

This corruption and lack of spirituality in the church led Lenin to view it as a parasite on society. He saw God as totally unnecessary in a modern world. He denied that spiritual longings existed in every human being—longings that needed fulfillment. Rather than seeing Christianity as the basis for morality and ethical behavior in society, he saw it as a challenge to the goals of the secular, humanistic state.

So Lenin developed a strategy to replace the church with Marxist philosophy. His desire was to replace the old structures with new ones, while avoiding confrontation, persecution, and repression as much as possible. His basic philosophy was, don't destroy something until you build something else.

With intensity and fury, he worked to develop a Marxist socialist state built on the achievements of workers. Although Lenin had pledged toleration, terror followed.

"Russia turned red with the blood of martyrs," says Pastor Gleb Yakunen, an orthodox priest devoted to religious freedom. The Communist Manifesto became the people's Bible, the leaders of the Communist Party their saints, and Lenin their savior.

After Lenin's death, Stalin took a much more aggressive approach in an attempt to destroy the church. He greatly accelerated the terror. In 1932 Stalin blew up one of the most beautiful Orthodox cathedrals in the southern part of Moscow, declaring Christianity dead. Stalin's repression of the church continued with fury. Christians were imprisoned, tortured, and sent to concentration camps by the notorious KGB.

Cautious historians estimate the death toll in the camps at 10-20 million. (Solzhenitsyn puts the figure at roughly 60-70 million.) In Stalin's era, over 40,000 priests are said to have lost their lives. Ninety-eight of every 100 orthodox churches were closed.

In his inspiring book *Pretenders to the Throne*, Roland Hegstad, editor of *Liberty* magazine, wrote:

> Of the 3,000 Seventh-day Adventists sent to prison camps only about 500 returned. Of 179 pastors sent into exile in 1929 only four returned.
>
> One old church member from Kiev, Galena, described the tragic situation this way: "One Sabbath, the police came during the church service. They took every grandfather, every father, every husband, every male over 18. We never saw them again. We were like a church without men. Wives without husbands. Children without fathers. Sisters without brothers. Through the years ours became a church of old women. Old women who never forgot, and who never forgot their faith in God or their hope of reunion someday."

The number of Christians who died during Stalin's repression is incomprehensible, yet reliable historical sources confirm the reality of that tragic era. Many Christians were committed to Christ during this time, and despite intense persecution, affirmed their faith in God.

In June of 1991, during our major evangelistic series in Moscow held in a university auditorium called the Plahanov Hall, I had an opportunity to become acquainted with many who were persecuted for their faith during the very difficult Stalin years.

I remember meeting with an old Babushka Russian grandmother. She invited my wife and I, along with Dr. and Mrs. D. Wayne Butcher, to eat at her home. As we arrived, we were totally embarrassed. She treated us like royalty. Though her home was simple and her belongings meager, the table was set beautifully. She brought out her best dishes for the occasion. The table was readied with an abundance of fruits and vegetables. She had baked pies and cakes for the occasion. Our meal, of course, began with traditional Russian borscht.

I estimated that the cost of the meal was probably two weeks of average salary. We felt badly that she would go to so much trouble and expense, yet her heart was open and hungry for spiritual fellowship. She had an inner zeal to discuss Christ and His love and the power of His Word.

As we sat eating, about halfway through the meal, I asked what I thought to be an innocent question. Have you ever asked a question and then immediately wished you could take it back? For me, this was one of those occasions. My question seemed simple and innocent to me, but for her it touched a vital nerve deep within her heart. It caused a memory to resurface she would like to have forgotten.

The question I asked was, "What was the most difficult experience you have ever had under Communism? Would you like to share with me the toughest experience you faced during the atheistic Communist years?"

Almost immediately, her lips began to quiver. Her hands trembled, her face reddened, and tears began to stream down her cheeks.

"I would like to forget it," she replied, "but I cannot. For many years, I attempted to teach my two daughters the principles of Christianity. I wanted them to know the Bible. I wanted them to know Jesus. I wanted them to know hymns that would bring them faith and encouragement. Here is one of my daughters," she said, gesturing toward a woman in her early 40s, "but the other is gone." The one daughter who was left smiled gently, and tears came also to her eyes and began running down her face as her mother continued.

"I knew we were being watched by the KGB, but each evening we would have family worship. Each evening I'd read to my girls from the Bible, and quietly and softly in the secrecy of our apartment, we would sing hymns. What I didn't know was that there was a KGB informer living above us. I saw KGB agents at times looking toward the apartment as I carefully pulled the curtains back and looked out the windows. We had attempted to be cautious. But the noose was tightening, and the KGB were watching us almost constantly.

"One evening after praying with my children, I gently tucked them into their beds. My older daughter was thirteen, and my younger daughter eleven. It was about one o'clock in the morning. We were all sleeping soundly, when I was awakened by the sound of heavy footsteps in the hall.

"Suddenly I heard a loud pounding on the door. Getting up, I cautiously opened the door. Two flashlights shone in my eyes. I couldn't see. Gradually, I recognized the three uniformed KGB officers. They pushed me aside, stormed into my apartment, and shook both of my daughters to awaken them.

"Then they took the younger one away, saying, 'This will teach you that there is only one acceptable order here, and that is Marxist Communism.' My daughter was crying and screaming—calling out 'Mama!' I watched as they took her out and slammed the door behind her. My 13-year-old daughter and I just stood there crying. And, Pastor, that was twenty-seven years ago, and I have never seen my 11-year-old daughter since. This was the price we paid for being Christians."

Silence gripped us. What could anyone say after such a poignant expression of faith? But finally I opened my heart and shared how thankful I was that Christ was coming again—and that one day this faithful mother and both of her daughters would be reunited.

If there is no God, if there is no faith, if there is no coming of Christ, then all the hopes and tears and prayers of the Soviet believers for seventy years are in vain. But God is real, and heaven is real, and the coming of Jesus is real!

I looked at this old Babushka, and lines were etched deeply into her face, yet it glowed with the serenity and peace of Christ. And I said to her, "You have experienced—and this country has experienced—seventy years of atheistic, godless Communism, but you have lived to see the fulfillment of Jesus' words in Matthew 24:14."

For there Christ said, "And this gospel of the kingdom shall be preached in all the world as a witness unto all nations, and then shall the end come." The last sign to be fulfilled before the coming of Jesus is the proclamation of the gospel to all the world. In Daniel 4:21, the prophet declared, "And He, God, changes the times and the seasons. He removes kings and sets up kings."

With one divine movement of His hand, God sweeps aside despotic regimes. He opens the doors of atheistic states. He removes totalitarian leaders. Christians see recent developments in the Soviet Union not simply as geopolitical events, but as the direct moving of God. He has opened the doors, and today a spiritual revolution is taking place.

As 1992 dawned, Seventh-day Adventist pastors planned to hold 187 evangelistic campaigns throughout the former

Soviet Union. In addition to these crusades, nearly sixty large city-wide evangelistic meetings were being planned by evangelists from Germany, Australia, England, and the United States.

During 1991, when the world headquarters of the Seventh-day Adventist Church launched a massive Soviet evangelistic thrust, over 50,000 attended evangelistic meetings, with nearly 12,000 people baptized.

People from all walks of life are accepting Christ's call to follow Him. One attorney told It Is Written evangelist Royce Williams, "Once I was like Saul. I persecuted this church. But now I know the truth. Thank you for what you have done for me."

A Soviet fighter pilot baptized in Riga, Latvia, told evangelist Jac Calon—at one time himself a U.S. Air Force captain who flew missions over North Viet Nam—"We were once mortal enemies who would have shot one another out of the sky, but now we are brothers in Christ."

Winfred Vogel, one of our German evangelists, continued his meetings even during the week of the coup. He tells of a university professor who stood up before the entire audience and asked, "Mr. Vogel, can you help me? I am teaching Marxism-Leninism, but my students do not listen to me anymore. They stare at the walls or out the window. What shall I do?"

After discussing the solid foundations of Christianity and the transforming power Jesus Christ brings into the life, Pastor Vogel invited this university professor to bring her students to the meetings as well. When the meetings ended, she, along with a number of them, was baptized.

In the mid-50s in Kiev, Khrushchev gave a devastating speech against Christianity. He ended his speech by emphatically declaring, "By the end of the century Christianity will be totally eradicated in the Soviet Union. But we are going to keep one Christian alive and bring him to Moscow and place him in a museum so people will know what a Christian looked like."

If only Khrushchev were alive today, how stunned he would be to discover that in the center of Moscow—in the heart of

the Kremlin, in the Communist Congress Party Hall—we have just completed a major evangelistic meeting with thousands in attendance.

The story of this book—the story of *The Cross and the Kremlin*—is Christ's story. It's the story of the tears and faith and perseverance and courage of Soviet Christians for seventy years. It's the story of God's moving in the heart of atheistic Communism to enable us to have an evangelistic meeting in the Kremlin. It's the story of a people's inner hunger for Bibles and of their desire to know God. It's the story of a revolution in Russia—a revolution far more meaningful from the perspective of eternity than the revolution that shook the world in October of 1917.

As you continue reading, your heart will thrill with a sense of what God is doing to finish His work in the world.

CHAPTER TWO

FROM CYNICS TO SEEKERS

As KLM Flight 301 touched down at Moscow's Sheremete Airport at 2:00 p.m. on March 11, 1992, my heart beat with eager anticipation. Although I had conducted evangelistic meetings throughout eastern Europe for the last seven years in such great cities as Budapest, Hungary; Belgrade, Yugoslavia; and Gdansk and Katovicie, Poland, I sensed that God was going to do something special in Moscow during this series of meetings.

At the invitation of the world headquarters of our church, I had been in Moscow less than a year earlier in June of 1991, when 3,000 people attended our evangelistic meetings and over 600 were baptized. During that visit I sensed that the Soviet Union was on the verge of a spiritual revolution. Never before in history had such an opportunity existed to win a nation for Christ.

Now, though my schedule was jammed, I felt that nothing was more important than preaching God's Word in this spiritually starved nation. Our entire Moscow team eagerly anticipated the mighty moving of God's Spirit. To be able to conduct an evangelistic meeting inside the Kremlin was a miracle indeed.

The word *Kremlin* comes from the Russian word *kreml*, which means "fortress." The Kremlin in Moscow is a triangular enclosure a mile and a half around and fortified by walls topped with towers. The present walls have stood since 1492. It's amazing to realize that the year Columbus discovered America, the walls of the Kremlin and its palaces were being built. What irony! Two nations, a world apart, that would ultimately develop two opposing philosophies: tyranny—and freedom.

The Kremlin today contains a bewildering number of complex buildings constructed over a wide span of history. As you enter the Kremlin, you're overwhelmed immediately by its magnificence and splendor. There you may see the old Imperial Palace—and five stately cathedrals. The Kremlin has been the center of Soviet culture for centuries.

Our evangelistic meetings were conducted in the Kremlin Palace Congress Hall—an absolutely magnificent building. Imported marble from the various Soviet republics was used in its construction. The main auditorium seats 6,000 people. Fourteen different escalators conveyed visitors to the meetings. In this great hall, Soviet films have been shown, ballet and theatrical productions performed, and Communist Party congresses held. A staff of over 500 people efficiently maintains the auditorium, which is impeccably clean. The top floor is an ornate banquet hall.

The opportunity to hold an evangelistic meeting in this formerly Communist Kremlin Palace Congress Hall was a providential turn of events indeed. Describing the Kremlin, Robert Spangler, coordinator for the Soviet Evangelistic Advance, wrote these words in the *Adventist Review* of June 4, 1992:

"From a political viewpoint the Kremlin, the capitol of

Communism for decades, is equal to our United States capitol. The major difference, the Kremlin Congressional Hall,

The Kremlin Palace Congress Hall has three balconies, fourteen escalators, and a staff of 500 to keep it running smoothly.

which seats 6,000 people, is used for secular as well as political events, but not for religious meetings."

I was overwhelmed to think that I would stand on the same

Over 12,000 jammed the Kremlin Congress Hall for two daily sessions.

platform where Khrushchev, Brezhnev, Andropov, Chernenko, and Gorbachev had delivered speeches on the atheistic philosophy of Marxism and open the Bible to share the gospel of Christ.

On the opening night of our Kremlin evangelistic meetings I visited briefly with Mikhail Kulakov, president of the Euro-Asia Division of Seventh-day Adventists, just before he introduced me. I was anxious to sense the emotions of this man of God, who had once been sentenced to life in exile for his faith.

"Pastor Kulakov," I asked, "had you ever considered the remote possibility that we would be holding an evangelistic meeting in the Kremlin?"

Tears welled up in his eyes, and his face brightened as he replied, "Pastor Finley, there was a time when we were afraid as Christians even to walk around the Kremlin. And now to think we have an evangelistic meeting *inside* the Kremlin—in the Congress Hall which has been the center of atheistic

The huge Kremlin Palace Congress Hall, seating 6,000, where two meetings were held daily, with a combined attendance of 12,000.

propaganda—is unbelievable to me."

I could tell by the emotion in his voice and the tears in his eyes that he was profoundly convinced God had worked mighty miracles. The overwhelming response to ticket sales indicated the spiritual hunger in the hearts of the people. Selling tickets for evangelistic meetings undoubtedly seems strange to us here in the United States. It certainly did to me! But the Kremlin officials required it as "the only way to control the crowds."

Two weeks before our evangelistic meetings were to begin, I received a fax from the coordinators of the evangelistic meetings in Moscow asking me urgently what they should do. All seats for the seven o'clock evening sessions were sold out.

We had made an agreement with the Kremlin officials that they would sell 4,500 seats in ticket outlets throughout Moscow. Thirteen hundred seats would be sold by our two Adventist churches. An additional thousand seats would be sold at the box office each day. Yet incredibly, two weeks before the evangelistic meetings, all except the box-office seats were sold.

We decided to go to a second session at three o'clock in the afternoon. Within a few days, every seat of the second session was sold as well. The only seats left were those to be purchased on the day of the meetings from the box office at the Kremlin Palace Hall. People stood in line for four hours to purchase seats.

Originally, seats for eleven meetings sold for five rubles. But speculators bought up the seats and jacked up the price to 100 rubles—or four day's pay—just before the evangelistic meetings started. The day of the meetings, seats were being hawked for 500 rubles for the eleven-meeting ticket. This factored out to two week's salary—or approximately $1,000 on the United States pay scale.

It was incredible to sense the hunger for the Word of God in this nation. If people would stand in line for four hours to get tickets—and be willing to pay the equivalent of two week's salary, what an evidence of the mighty, miraculous moving of the Spirit of God!

Truly a spiritual hunger exists in the heart and life of every human being—a hunger that cannot be satisfied except through the presence of Jesus Christ. Jesus stated an eternal truth in Matthew 4:4 when He said, "Man shall not live by bread alone, but by every word that proceeds out of the mouth of God."

Communism offered people bread, food, and housing—but it neglected their inner, spiritual needs. The Soviet Union was a spiritually bankrupt nation filled with people longing to know Christ. Today its people hunger for the moral and ethical principles of God's Word.

As we arrived at the airport prior to the meetings and went through customs formalities, our hosts greeted us warmly. They informed me that shortly we had an interview at the Moscow Journalist's Club. The Moscow Journalist's Club is not known for its friendship toward either Americans or evangelists. By profession, journalists tend to be a skeptical, cynical group, and I wondered what to expect. For many Christians, the Moscow Journalist's Club is reminiscent of the story of Daniel. You feel as if you're being thrown to the lions. I wondered what would happen.

As we arrived, we were welcomed warmly and greeted with flowers and open arms. The atmosphere was pleasant. The Moscow Journalist's Club is housed in a 200-year-old building of careful artistic detail located in a magnificent section of Moscow.

Between twenty and twenty-five journalists—TV reporters, magazine and newspaper editors, and magazine writers—were present. I opened the news conference with a short explanation of why we were there. I discussed the fact that every country needs a moral basis for its society—and that without such a foundation, any society will eventually crumble.

Leaders of the new Commonwealth of Independent States

have recently been calling for this moral ethic. Communism has not provided a basis for morality in society. As a result, robbery, murder, drugs, prostitution, and both political and social corruption are rampant. Leaders have voiced the fear of a total collapse of their society, leading to rebellion and anarchy, unless they can find a way to change the very heart of their social system. They have emphasized the need to change the direction of society and to establish it on a firm moral basis.

In January of 1992, my wife and I attended the National Religious Broadcasters Association meetings held at the Sheraton Inn in Washington, D.C. A group of high-level officials from the former Soviet Union attended those meetings. The group consisted of Anatoli Tupikin, Chairman of Russian National Radio and Television; Vladimir Zots, Special Assistant and advisor to former Soviet President Mikhail Gorbachev; and Constantine Lubenchenko, former Chairman of the Supreme Soviet and now President of the Parliament Center and counselor to the Constitutional Court of Russia.

In that meeting before religious broadcasters throughout America, Dr. Zots said, "In our country today we're experiencing spiritual revolution, and I'm thoroughly convinced that no changes are going to be meaningful in our society unless they be spiritual changes."

A few minutes later, Anatoli Tupikin took the platform and said, "I believe with all my heart that without this book, the Bible, man cannot live in current society."

Ten years ago, when the U.S.S.R. was still a dominant superpower, Aleksandr Solzhenitsyn spoke forcibly of the need to return to God in his nation. In his famed 1983 Templeton address, he declared, "If I were asked today to formulate as concisely as I could the possible main cause of the ruinous revolution that swallowed up some 60 million of our people, I could not put it more accurately than, 'men have forgotten God.'"

At the Journalist's Club, I was impressed, after my presentation on Christianity and the Bible as the basis for morality and ethics, that the Soviet journalists were wide open to considering the Bible as a basis for morality in society. Their questions were not cynical or skeptical—they were the questions of seekers. They queried honestly, "How do you see Christianity as making a meaningful change in the life of people? How does the Bible relate to life? How do you develop faith? How can a man or a woman experiencing

Pastor Finley addressing the journalists. They seemed more like honest seekers than cynical skeptics.

bitterness or anger find forgiveness in Christianity?"

These questions reminded me of a television interview about nine months before on "Good Evening Moscow." A woman some considered to be "the Barbara Walters of the Soviet Union" had invited me to appear on the program, which runs each evening from seven to ten on prime time on

Moscow's popular Channel 2. It is one of the most-viewed programs in the country and has a viewing audience of between thirty and forty million.

The interview was conducted in the communications center of the Soviet Union—the former citadel of atheistic propaganda. As we arrived, we were given a special pass and ushered past Soviet soldiers and guards, through a maze of corridors, into Channel 2's television studio.

Waiting for my interviewer, I wondered what kinds of questions she would ask. The hostess who prepared me for the interview asked, "Mr. Finley, you're a clergyman, aren't you?"

"Yes, I am," I responded.

"Are you a pastor?"

"Yes."

"Do you do occasional counseling?"

"Certainly."

"The interviewer tonight is deeply troubled," she continued. "She has had some personal problems in her family—in her home—and her heart is just bleeding from what she's been through. Can you give her some words of encouragement tonight?"

I silently prayed, "Lord, please help me to help this interviewer. Please help me know what to say and how to say it. Help me bring some words of hope and encouragement to her."

As I sat there silently praying that I would have a few minutes with her before the program began, time raced on. We only had a minute now before the program was to begin, and the interviewer had not yet appeared. I wondered if she was so distraught that she wouldn't appear that night. A few seconds before the interview, she walked out and said, "Mr. Finley, I'm glad to meet you, but it's time for our interview to begin."

I noticed the redness in her eyes. Quickly her associates

combed her hair and put a little extra makeup on her. Suddenly the cameras were rolling. We were on live. There was just no time for any words of counsel. She asked about the meetings and about the impact of Christ and the Bible on human lives.

And then, spontaneously, she asked, "What if a person came to you and asked for counsel? What if they were filled with bitterness and anger because they had terrible family problems? How could you help a person who had such bitterness or anger toward somebody else?"

Instantly the spiritual impact of the question hit me. This woman was opening her heart to me before thirty-five million people! The question wasn't for somebody else. It was for her. She had been hurt and bruised, and she needed help.

I talked about the reality of that hurt and about the reality of the anger that develops within us when we're hurt. I pointed out to her that to deny this is to destroy our spiritual health. And then I talked about Jesus, who was betrayed by His friends and rejected by those for whom He came to die. I recalled that as He was being crucified, as nails were being driven through His hands, as a crown of thorns was jammed upon His head, as blood ran down His face, and as a spear pierced His side, He had prayed, "Father, forgive them, for they don't understand what they're doing."

And as we talked before an audience of millions, I sensed the Spirit of God coming into that television studio. I sensed that Christ Himself was speaking about forgiveness, about mercy, about lancing the boil of bitterness and resentment. Christ was appealing in that studio to that interviewer of the Communist state to forgive her offender.

After the program ended, the hostess was visibly shaken—so much so that she broke down and began to cry and had to leave the set. While she was gone, the program director came over to me and said, "During your answer about bitterness and anger, the cameramen were crying. The people in charge of lighting and sound were crying." And she added, "There is a different atmosphere in this place."

Soon my interviewer returned, expressing heartfelt thanks for the love of Christ that had brought forgiveness. And there in that center of Communism, in that atheistic communications system, we gathered in a circle and prayed. We asked the Lord to grant peace and forgiveness within. I took a Russian Bible out of my briefcase and gave it to my interviewer, encouraging her to read the Psalms and discover the peace they can bring. As I quoted Psalm 91, I could see that she was visibly touched: "He that dwelleth in the secret place of the Most High shall abide under the shadow of the Almighty. I will say of the Lord, He is my refuge and my fortress, my God; in Him will I trust."

"Christ is a mighty refuge," I told her. "You can trust Him. You can flee to the security of His arms."

She reached out, took my hand, and said, "Tonight I'm going to be in church. I need to find the peace and security that Christ can bring."

Remembering my experience with this television interviewer, recalling her openness to the gospel and the practicality of her questions, I was now impressed again at the Journalist's Club with the openness of the journalists. What atheists had attempted to destroy, thinking men and women throughout Russian society desperately needed.

The Bible is not some finespun theological treatise, but practical counsel on what it really means to be a Christian. And the Russian people need help in learning how to study the Bible. They need help understanding who Jesus is and how to live Christian lives. They need help to know how the doctrines of Scripture can be applied to daily life. They need to know whether Christianity makes a difference, and if so, how?

During that entire interview with the journalists, not one skeptical, cynical, or theoretical question arose. What they wanted to know was what every human being needs to know: How can I know God? How can I be saved in His kingdom? How can I live with Him forever?

I opened my heart and told them about the living Christ—and about how Jesus came down from heaven to live the perfect life we should have lived. The human race had been separated from God and deserved eternal death, but that Christ had entered into the grave and paid the penalty for sin.

Christ perfectly reflected the love of God. The greatest revelation of love in the universe is Jesus. This world is so filled with hate and bitterness that we need a revelation—a model—of that love. And I stressed that we also need the transforming grace of Christ to bring us into harmony with that love.

Before those journalists, I said, "You know, Communism had some positive ideals, but the problem is that the nature of man is fallen." I shared with them Jeremiah 17:9, which says, "The heart of man is deceitful above all things and desperately wicked: who can know it?"

The prophet also asked who could bring a clean thing out of an unclean. I pointed out to those journalists that the heart of man is fallen, that his nature is corrupt, and that without Jesus Christ there is no possibility for moral change. But Jesus died to pay the penalty for our sins—to deliver us from guilt and fear. And He is resurrected—He's alive. This living Christ can transform our lives, change our hearts, and make us over again. To that living Christ, those journalists responded. But then they asked me a question I wasn't prepared for at all—a question that stopped me in my tracks. The question stunned me.

"Mr. Finley," they asked, "what is your opinion of the article that came out in *Izvestia* this week? How will you relate to the Communist rally scheduled for March 17—a day when the Communists want to enter the Kremlin Palace Congress Hall and hold their rally, but cannot because you are in that auditorium? How will you relate to that?"

Their question was but a preview of dramatic events that would soon place us at the center of an international political conflict.

CHAPTER THREE

BUSH, LEAVE OUR SOULS ALONE!

On March 10, 1992—the day before our meeting with the Moscow Journalist's Club—*Izvestia*, one of Moscow's two leading newspapers and boasting a circulation of over four million, ran a news story headlined "COMMUNISTS' DESIRE TO HOLD RALLY IN KREMLIN CONGRESS HALL THWARTED."

The article noted the upcoming rally on March 17 of the hard-line Communist faction in and around Red Square. They desired to lead their supporters through the Trotsky gate in the Kremlin to conduct the rally in their former Communist Party Congress Hall. According to the article, Kremlin officials informed them that a meeting on March 17 in the auditorium would be impossible, since an American Seventh-day Adventist evangelist was holding a series of lectures entitled "The Bible in the Kremlin" in that auditorium. Here is an exact Russian translation of this amazing article, which thrust us into the center of a political storm:

> It was announced on March 9 during the session of the Supreme Soviet of the Russian Federation that the former peoples' deputies of the U.S.S.R. are planning to conduct their session in the usual place for them, the Kremlin Congressional Hall. This information caused amazement to the leadership of the Kremlin Congressional Hall. The administrator, Anatoli Elsfov, said to the *Izvestia* reporter that the peoples' deputies of the U.S.S.R. have not applied to the director for renting the hall.

The news story continued with this amazing statement:

> In the schedule of the Palace there is planned for March 14-25 another activity entitled, "Biblical Way to New Life." It will be conducted by American Seventh-day Adventists.

In the providence of God, newspapers, radio, and television catapulted this story across the former U.S.S.R. The question the journalists raised in our news conference the next day sought to learn how we would relate to the hard-line Communist rally on March 17.

For a moment I was stunned. To think that the Communists could not return to their Congress Hall because we were conducting an evangelistic meeting there was truly incredible. And that the democratic forces within the former Soviet Union appreciated the fact that we were there and refused to let the Communists go back into their hall was astonishing! This was a miracle of miracles. Trying to regain my composure before those journalists, I hesitated and then made this observation: The ethic of pure Communism is to establish a just, moral, society—a society filled with contented, happy, healthy, citizens who are part of a peaceful world. Communism's failures occurred in at least two major areas.

First, it failed to recognize that since human beings are intrinsically selfish, it is impossible for them to carry out the ideal of love in a society. Self-centered human beings will grasp whatever they can for themselves, to protect their self-interest. A godless society will be filled with power struggles, dishonesty, and a lack of moral direction, unless the living Christ provides divine power from above. One of the fundamental shortcomings of Communism is that it not only fails to provide a moral ethic for society, it also fails to provide any moral power for change. Second, even if some within the Communist structure may appear to be good, moral people, atheistic Communism provides no hope for a life after death. It doesn't answer such basic questions of life as "Where did I come from?" "What's the real purpose of life?" or "How can I live forever?"

Our Bible lectures in the Kremlin, I went on, will attempt to present both the basis for morality in society and the basis for personal moral change through the power of the living Christ. They will provide people with hope for today because they know that their future is bright tomorrow. They can face the future with confidence.

The religious philosopher Emil Brunner once said, "Man can survive anything if he has hope. What oxygen is to the lungs, hope is to the yearning spirit."

If all we have to look forward to is economic depression, a sickly body, and a poverty-stricken society, we have nothing—absolutely nothing. And if all human beings have to look forward to is the grave, there is absolutely no hope. But Christianity gives hope to men and women today, because it provides a vision of tomorrow which is genuine and optimistic. It provides men and women with the hope of eternal life and eternal heaven. And they need that hope in a poverty-stricken society.

A story that used to make the rounds in Moscow helps us understand how grim economic conditions really are. The story would begin by asserting that Adam and Eve were Russians. Then someone would protest, "What do you mean, Adam and Eve were Russians? That sounds ridiculous!"

"Well," the storyteller would explain, "it's a logical deduction. They were improperly clothed, they possessed only one apple between them, and someone was always telling them that they lived in paradise."

But today nobody is telling the Russians they live in paradise. Long lines, food shortages, and a severe housing crunch all indicate that something is terribly wrong. In their minds, Communism is dead. The seventy-year experiment with atheistic Communism has left their nation both morally and economically bankrupt.

This assessment, however, was not shared by the hard-line Communists left in Moscow. These power-hungry officials were fighting for their lives. And in the rally scheduled for Red Square on March 17, 1991, they saw what might be a final opportunity to amass popular support for the return of Communism. They hoped to mobilize at least 100,000 people for the rally. But we stood in the way of their accomplishing their ultimate goal of marching back into the Kremlin Congress Hall through the Trotksy gate.

When we opened our evangelistic meetings on Saturday,

People streamed through the Trotsky gate to enter the Kremlin for the evangelistic meetings. Lenin entered this gate in 1917, proclaiming the Communist state.

March 14, at 3:00 p.m., hundreds and hundreds streamed over the drawbridge through the Trotsky gate to attend. In two separate sessions on our opening day of the meetings, more than 12,000 people jammed the Kremlin Palace Congress Hall. As I stood before the huge throng and saw the eager anticipation registered in their eyes and on their faces, my heart rejoiced. Their hearts were opened, and they responded with warm applause to the presentations. The Spirit of God was obviously present in the auditorium. Political leaders, scientists, educators, sociologists, physicians, researchers, economists, as well as factory owners were present that night. An unusually high class and representative cross section of society were in attendance.

After the meeting, a top public official visited me in my private dressing room, along with a former high-ranking military officer who had played a prominent role in the Afghan invasion.

As we talked together, this official looked me in the eye and said, "Mr. Finley, I was here when Brezhnev spoke and when Khrushchev spoke. I was here when Andropov and Chernenko spoke. And of course, I was here when Mikhail Gorbachev and Boris Yeltsin debated over the future of our society. But tonight as I listened to you speak, I sensed that what you said about the need for moral change and the need for a new society based on biblical principles of honesty is exactly what our country needs today. My heart responds to your call for this new spiritual direction."

Then the officer—a huge, imposing man—reached for my hand. As he squeezed it, I was thankful he was my friend and not my enemy. I imagined him attempting to give me a Russian bearhug and crushing every bone in my body. His deep, pensive eyes revealed a man of inner conviction and thought.

"Take this comment from a military man," he said. "We had hoped for victory in Afghanistan, but we did not achieve it. Yet tonight, the fact that you opened the Word of God in the Kremlin and shared Christ here—this is victory!"

As the two men left, my heart was filled a sense of the

presence of Christ. I knelt in my little backstage room and said, "Thank You, God. This was indeed victory tonight. Your Word was proclaimed here in the stronghold of atheism, and hearts and minds were touched."

A knock on my door interrupted my prayer. It was my translator, Peter Kulakov.

"Mark," he said, "there are two television crews waiting to interview you. Can you come immediately?"

Channel 1 and Channel 2—two of the most powerful television stations in the entire country, with a viewing audience of millions—were eager for an interview. As I came out for the interview, one of the first questions asked was, "How

The Evening News with Channels 1 and 2, covering 35 to 40 million people, featured the meetings regularly.

do you react to the demonstration by the Communists going on outside right now?"

"What do you mean?" I responded. "I'm unaware that a demonstration is taking place."

"Oh, yes," a television reporter replied. "A major demonstration against you is going on right now. The crowd is holding up signs that say, BUSH, LEAVE OUR SOULS ALONE, and AMERICAN IMPERIALISM. In fact, the demonstrators are quite nasty at times to people coming into the meetings."

Whatever accusations the demonstrators brought against

us, we had come to reach out in the love of Christ to the community and would not openly condemn them. They have a right to demonstrate, I told the reporter. But if indeed they desire moral change for the nation, they should present a plan to bring about that moral change. Our goal is to reach out through the power of the living Christ to achieve and realize moral change.

Immediately after the interview, I gathered some of my Russian pastors together and asked, "Has anybody been out in the streets tonight? And what is the situation?"

Pastor Michael Kaminsky spoke up immediately. "Yes, I've been out in the streets. I've been trying to aid our people to get into the meeting. And the situation is rather serious. Placards are being held up. A group is waving Russian flags in support of a return to Russian nationalism. But probably the most serious thing, Mark, is that some have marched with your picture in a black frame. Do you understand what that means?"

"Why, no, I'm not certain."

"It means death to the one whose picture is in the frame." Momentarily, my stomach tightened and a lump formed in my throat. But then almost immediately my mind went to 1 John 4:18: "There is no fear in love, but perfect love casts out fear, because fear has torment."

And I began thinking, "If God has sent you to Russia, there is no need to fear. If He hasn't sent you, then you had better take the next plane home tomorrow. Didn't God arrange for the evangelistic meetings to be held in the Kremlin? Didn't He open the doors of freedom in this country? Didn't He place it within the hearts of over 12,000 people to attend this meeting tonight? And if God could take care of Daniel in Babylon and Joseph in Egypt, He can certainly take care of you in Moscow. Go home tonight and sleep well."

Some suggested that we not stay in our rooms that night—

that instead we switch rooms. But, I thought, if I live in fear, constantly switching rooms, this indicates defeat for God, not victory. So I decided to ask the Lord to send angels to protect me. And I asked that if somebody wanted to take my life, God would miraculously intervene. I reminded Him that I was not there on a pleasure trip, but on His assignment.

After the meeting, I went home and went to sleep—and slept soundly. The next day there were no demonstrations at our meetings, nor did any occur on Monday. Thousands continued to attend. As Tuesday approached, we knew this could be a significant day in the history of the world.

The Communists had planned this massive demonstration rally for six months. They hoped to rally at least a hundred thousand people in the streets—maybe more. They also hoped that this show of power—a blatant call for a return to Communism—would totally overwhelm the Yeltsin government and lead to its collapse.

I was sitting in the twenty-first-floor restaurant of the Russia Hotel with our staff, eating my lunch, when three of my colleagues entered: Neal Wilson, former president of the General Conference of Seventh-day Adventists, and now in charge of Soviet affairs; Robert Spangler, evangelistic coordinator for Soviet affairs; and Mikhail Kulakov, president of the Euro-Asia Division.

They too were going to eat, but first they wanted to spend a few moments talking with me. They were serious and candid as they told me they had received information from high-ranking officials in the government that the demonstration on March 17 might bring bloodshed. No one, it seemed, really knew what was going to happen. And they were concerned—concerned about my personal safety, and also about what might happen to the people trying to get into the evangelistic meetings at the same time that maybe a hundred thousand people were rallying in the streets.

We greatly appreciated the earnestness of Pastors Wilson, Spangler, and Kulakov. They apprised us of the seriousness of the situation, yet left any decision about possibly canceling the meeting on Tuesday night to us. They applied no pressure whatsoever, but gave us Godly counsel.

I knew that the decision was mine, and I wondered what to do. It was not concern for my personal safety, but rather concern for the safety of the 10- to 12 thousand people coming to the meetings that caused me serious reflection. If people coming to the meetings met the demonstrators head on and there was bloodshed, I would feel personally responsible. Yet if we canceled the meeting and the hall was empty, what position would that put the Kremlin officials in? Those democratic forces, who had already pointed out to the Communists that they could not use the hall because we were there, would be openly embarrassed.

After praying about it, I decided to approach the top leadership of the Kremlin Congress Hall and ask them for counsel. Early Monday afternoon, I arrived at the Kremlin. The guards, recognizing me, opened the gates and let me through. I had asked for an appointment with the administrator of the Congress Hall. We took the elevator to the fifth floor and wound down narrow corridors until we came to his office. I came immediately to the point.

"Sir, in light of the fact that there will be a massive demonstration tomorrow and that some public officials are predicting bloodshed, is it wise for us to have an evangelistic meeting in the Kremlin tomorrow?

"I'm considering canceling the meeting—not because of my personal safety, but for the safety of the attendees at the meeting. Do you feel their lives would be in danger if they came to the meeting tomorrow night in the Kremlin?"

Without hesitation, the administrator responded.

"As far as your personal safety is concerned, the general

of the army in charge of security in the Kremlin assures me that you are in absolutely no danger at all. And as for your attendees, we will have hundreds of troops in the streets. They will be massed between the demonstrators and those coming to the meeting, keeping the two groups separated. Tell your people to take the underground immediately to the Trotsky gate and to come right up through the gate—and our soldiers will keep them separated. We want to assure you that your people will be safe in the Kremlin."

In my mind, the decision was made. We were going to go on with the meeting. It was going to be a victory for God's cause. As I left that administrator, my heart rejoiced. And I thought to myself, How God confounds the enemy! How Christ confuses the devil's forces! Here the Soviet army is holding Communist demonstrators back so that 10,000 people can come and hear the Bible preached in the Kremlin. Talk about a mighty miracle!

The Communists are locked outside the walls, and we are inside the walls of the Kremlin protected by the army in order to have an evangelistic meeting. How mighty and great is our God! What a fulfillment of Habakkuk 1:5: "Behold ye among the heathen [or the atheists] and regard and wonder marvelously; for I will work a work in your days which you will not believe though it is told you."

God's miracles are truly unbelievable. And the days of such miracles are not over.

CHAPTER FOUR

THE WILL OF THE PEOPLE

Our meeting in the Kremlin Congress Hall started normally on Monday night, March 16. The all-Russian choir sang magnificently. As Dr. Walter Thompson rose to give his medical presentation prior to my sermon, a man in about the fourth row back on the left jumped up and began shouting in Russian.

Immediately I turned to my translator and asked, "Peter, what's going on?" Attempting to decipher the shouting, he responded, "Mark, he's asking Dr. Thompson how you will relate to the Communist demonstration tomorrow. He desires a public statement of support for that Communist rally before these 6,000 people." Standing at the microphone, Dr. Thompson hesitated. I whispered, "Walt, go on with your presentation. Ignore him." But the man was not to be ignored.

"I ask you again," he demanded, "what is your feeling toward the Communist demonstration? Make a public statement." Again I whispered, "Walt, go on with your presentation."

But it was impossible. By this time the man was shouting, "The will of the people! The will of the people! The will of the people!" In other words, according to this man, it was the will of the people that we make a public statement supporting Communism.

At that point, my mind in a whirl, I silently prayed, asking God what we should do next. But then a great chorus of voices swept like a tidal wave over the hall as more than 6,000 people began shouting, "Carry him out! Carry him out! Carry him out!" And four strong ushers walked down the aisle, put their arms around this one lone Communist in the crowd, and carried him out!

What irony! He was shouting for the will of the people, and the people expressed their will. They carried him out. The will of the people in Russia is not Communism. It's not atheism. It's not godless materialism. The will of the people today in the former Soviet Union seems to be a longing for deep spiritual values. They long to know God. They have a heart desire to know the truths of the Bible.

Why else would people stand in line for four hours to get tickets to meetings entitled "The Bible in the Kremlin"? Why would they jostle and push to receive the free Bibles we offered? Why would they spend hours—some of them up to six a day—studying their Bibles? Only one reason. The Holy Spirit has moved powerfully to create a desire for God and truth and Scripture within their hearts and minds.

Each evening at our evangelistic meetings, we offered a free Bible to any who would attend a minimum of four times. An attendance control card was issued to each person, and ushers punched the cards as people came into the meeting each night. Once they had four punches in their cards, they qualified for a free Bible.

We began distributing those Bibles the fifth night. Hundreds upon hundreds lined up to get their free copy of the Bible. Now, in order for them to qualify for a free Bible, it

Some of the hundreds who lined up to receive their free Bible.

was necessary not only for them to come four nights, but to commit themselves to completing a 24-lesson Bible course that we had translated into Russian.

I had used this approach in my previous evangelistic meetings at the Plahanov Institute in June of 1991. When I had then suggested to the pastors that we give out a free Bible with lessons to people willing to do them, the pastors objected strongly. They said, "Mark, you don't know the Russian people. They will try to get two, three, four, or five Bibles. They will take your Bibles and sell them on the streets. Once you begin giving out Bibles without charging money for them, you will totally lose control of the situation, and there will be chaos."

They suggested we charge 35 rubles for a Bible—the

equivalent of one day's pay. My heart was broken. It was impossible for me to be honest with my own soul—with my own conscience—and yet charge a day's pay for a Bible, knowing that these people had not had an opportunity to receive a Bible for seventy years. Knowing that many Christians had hand copied a page or two of the Bible and been imprisoned for it. Knowing that many of them had suffered for having a Bible in their possession. And knowing that most families do not have a Bible.

I could not conceivably think of charging them for a Bible. I told my Russian pastors in that earlier crusade that I was going to go before the people and tell them exactly what the pastors had said. And we agreed that I would develop a covenant sheet—a contract between the individual receiving the Bible and his Lord.

My announcement to the audience went something like this: "We have been told that we can't trust you—that if we give you Bibles, you'll take three or four, or steal them, or go out and sell them when you receive them—that you really do not so much have a great desire to study the Bible as to get something free."

The audience was stunned that I would be so blunt with them. But I continued.

"We really believe in you. We believe that you want a copy of the Bible to study personally. And we're prepared to give you a copy."

At this point the entire audience of thousands broke into a thunderous, continuous applause. Their hearts were deeply moved to think someone would give them a Bible.

"But there are two conditions to receiving this Bible," I went on. "Are you willing to follow them? First, we can only give one Bible to a person. And to indicate your seriousness in studying the Bible, you must be here four nights before you qualify to receive your Bible. Second, I have a contract drawn up that says you are committing yourself before God to do Bible lessons if you receive a copy of the Bible. We are prepared to give you a Bible if you are prepared to study it."

Again, thousands of people responded in Russian, saying "Da, da, da." Which meant yes, yes, yes—give us the Bibles, and we will study them.

Moscow University did a careful statistical analysis and sociological study on the people coming to our meetings. They discovered that sixty-five percent of all the households represented did not have a Bible before the meetings began. But ninety-two percent of the people received a Bible. And ninety-six percent of those still coming to the meetings three weeks later were doing the Bible course.

The will of the people today in the former Soviet Union is to study the Bible and to find spiritual reality. And what a difference the Word of God makes in the lives of those who will study it. Paul stated it well in Hebrews 4:12, when he said, "The word of God is living and powerful, and sharper than any two edged sword."

The principles of God's Word carry with them creative power. David, in Psalm 33:6, said, "By the word of the Lord are the heavens made and all the host of them by the breath of His mouth. He spoke and it was done. He commanded and it stood fast."

The Psalmist David declared that there is creative power in God's Word. When God spoke, the darkness was chased away by light. His Word brought life out of nothingness. He spoke—and Earth was carpeted with living green. Flowers of every color and shape and variety bloomed and blossomed. Fruit trees brought forth fruit in abundance.

In Eden when God spoke, birds and animals and fishes appeared. And as the crowning act in creation, He created human life. God's Word is so powerful that as He speaks, the audible word creates tangible matter. The syllables that go out of God's mouth are creative syllables—they create whatever they declare.

Ellen White comments in the book *Education*, page 126: "The creative energy that called the world into existence is in the word of God."

When men and women study the Bible. their hearts and minds and lives are totally, completely transformed.

One night I was seated in my study between meetings in an industrial hall called ZVI. After our evangelistic meetings left their Kremlin location, we began preaching in other auditoriums throughout the city. Our total evangelistic process lasted six weeks. Between evangelistic meetings, the door suddenly burst open, and a rugged-looking Russian walked in. He began speaking loudly and gesturing. His eyes were deeply set in his face, and his long hair and bearded face revealed a certain roughness.

At first, I thought that something I might have said in the meetings had angered him. It appeared that he desired to physically harm me. My translator stood between the two of us. I couldn't understand a word he was saying, but something had him agitated.

My translator turned to me and said, "Mark, this man has come to the meetings. He has been coming to both sessions—at three and again at seven. He doesn't want to miss a meeting.

"He's been a prisoner in the Russian prisons. He tells of the horrible conditions in the prisons and of the terrible, abominable filth and squalor. But he speaks now of accepting Christ and of the joy Jesus has given him. Yet he is filled with guilt and fear because of his past sin. He has been in prison for years and has just been released.

"His question to you is, 'How can I be free from guilt? How can I have peace of mind?'"

I asked the man to be seated, and we talked of Jesus—His birth, His life, and His death. I read to him Romans 3:23: "All have sinned and come short of the glory of God." I pointed out that guilt is a universal problem. And then we read Romans 6:23: "The wages of sin is death, but the gift of God is eternal life through Jesus Christ our Lord." I then added Ephesians 2:8: "By grace are you saved through faith, and that not of yourselves. It is the gift of God. Not of works, lest any man should boast."

As the principles of the Word of God lodged in this prisoner's mind, I noticed his eyes beginning to sparkle, and a smile came over his face. He sensed that salvation was his as a gift. He sensed that God was a God of pardon and mercy and forgiveness.

We knelt together on the floor of that little study. We put our arms around one another as I prayed a simple prayer. "Dear Father, Peter is coming to you right now. He desires Your forgiveness, Your peace, Your freedom from guilt. Oh, God, grant him through the name of Jesus Christ Your grace and pardon and forgiveness. And I believe that You will, because You've said that if we confess our sins, You are faithful and just to forgive them. Thank You that You'll do that right now, dear Lord. And that You will grant this brother forgiveness through Jesus Christ our Lord. Amen."

I then tapped him on the shoulder and said, "Peter, you pray." Peter had never prayed before. As he opened his heart to Jesus, his lips began to quiver. His entire body began to shake. Tears ran down his face as he prayed, "Oh, Jesus, please forgive me. Oh, Jesus, I'm filled with guilt. Please pardon me."

When we arose from our knees, he threw his arm around me and hugged me. He was a new man. The peace of Christ filled his life. Peter received God's forgiveness that night. His guilt was gone. Thousands more have gathered at the cross. They have come to Jesus and experienced the inner healing my new Russian friend Peter experienced—a freedom from the accusing voices of the past. If you have not experienced this inner oneness with Christ, you can experience it too. His arms are wide open for you. God miraculously touched the life of this prisoner, and He can touch your life too!

Today throughout the former Soviet Union, it is the will of the vast majority of the people to know God! Their will is to understand the Bible. Their will is to have a meaningful relationship with Jesus Christ. For many, many years they were oppressed against their will.

Consider Anna. Anna was brought up in the Ukraine in a Christian home. Her father and mother cautiously and quietly shared the principles of God's Word with her. And when Anna was in her thirties, she made a decision to spend much of her life secretly copying the Bible and sharing those secret pages with anyone who willing to read or listen.

Anna was a seamstress. She sewed thick quilts and put them in her closet as wall coverings. She got a special table and a little old plunkety-plunk typewriter, which she put in that closet. Day after day, with very dim light, Anna typed the Bible in her closet.

As a change of scenery, she made a great covering for her dining-room table and hung it over the table. Day after day she would go under that table and sit there with her typewriter. Again, plunkety plunk, plunking away—copying the Bible. She spent eight hours a day, day in and day out, week in and week out, month in and month out, copying the Word of God. She made six copies at a time.

As she continued her copying, she looked for trusted seekers after truth with whom to share her precious copies. Anna continued her copying work for twenty years. Hundreds and hundreds of her neighbors received new hope and courage from her copies of the Bible. But after twenty years of copying in dim light under terrible circumstances, Anna went blind.

Yet today, because of her prayers and labor and tears, and because of the faithfulness of hundreds of other Annas, God has opened the doors of the former Soviet Union—and the

Filming on location—directly in front of the KGB building—the gripping story of Anna, whose daughter was seized as a child by the KGB.

light shines forth clearly. One thing is certain: It is the will of the people today to hear God's Word and to know His will.

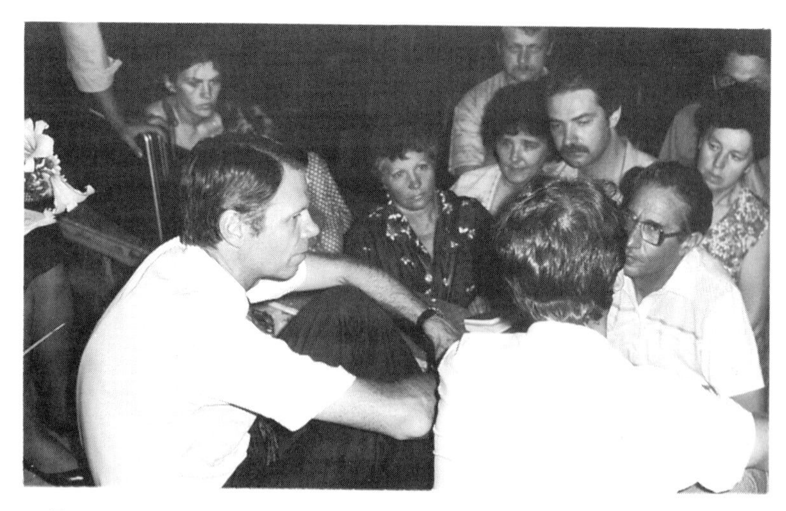

Eager crowds thronged Pastor Finley with their questions after each meeting.

CHAPTER FIVE

STORIES OF CHANGED LIVES

Does any evidence exist demonstrating that Christianity makes a significant difference in people's lives? From a sociological standpoint, do Christians have better family relationships? Do they have better relationships in the workplace? Are their emotions more positive and joyful? Do they have a greater inner peace and less depression and anxiety?

For seventy years, atheistic communism has claimed that Christianity is mere wish fulfillment. Communist philosophers have alleged that Christianity is a crutch—totally unnecessary in a modern, sophisticated society.

When representatives from the Sociology Department at Moscow University approached me and asked if I would be interested in studying the changes in the lives of people who had come to our evangelistic meetings, I was delighted. I recognized that this university department was an objective think tank.

If changes in human lives could be quantified, this would

have a powerful effect on the influence of Christianity throughout the entire Soviet Union.

Dr. Alexander T. Gasparishvili is the deputy director for the Public Opinion Research Center, the Faculty of Sociology, Moscow University. Dr. Gasparishvili was also a visiting lecturer on the Sociology of Russia at Yale University in New Haven, Connecticut. Along with his capable research assistant, Varzanova Tatyana, he agreed to do a complete sociological study of the people coming to our evangelistic meetings.

Now, we had one advantage. Tatyana had attended the Bible presentations I held previously in Plahanov Hall and was deeply impressed. Spiritual changes were taking place in her own life. She felt that similar changes were taking place in other people's lives.

Dr. Gasparishvili was not as sure. He approached the survey feeling that there might be some change in some lives, but that such change certainly would not be very remarkable, much less demonstrable.

We met three times before the survey was taken. We agreed that it would be taken during the fourth and fifth weeks of our six-week series. This would provide adequate time to demonstrate any possible changes. We also agreed that we needed between 1,000 and 1,500 completed surveys to obtain an adequate sample group for measuring lifestyle changes.

The survey consisted of thirty-seven different questions, measuring attitudes, feelings, emotions, and lifestyle practices—as well as doctrinal understanding. It was conducted on April 5 and 6. Our sample group consisted of 1,169 people. The results of the survey, in Dr. Gasparishvili's own words, were astounding.

"I expected some change," he said, "but certainly nothing like what we found. I didn't think your lectures would be nearly so effective, and the results are much higher than we expected."

We discovered that during the meetings, 92.4 percent of the people were actively reading their Bible. Ninety-six percent began doing our Bible lessons.

What impact did this have on their lifestyles? What impact did this have on their thinking processes? Negative emotions such as fear, anxiety, depression, and worry were reduced tenfold. Positive emotions increased two to three times. Ninety-one percent of those coming to the meetings said that they had realized positive changes in their lives. Attendees were 200 percent less likely to smoke and 300 percent less likely to drink. Sixty-five percent of the attendees said they had more positive family relationships as a result of attending the meetings. Forty percent said their efficiency at work and their work relationships had improved as a result of the meetings.

In short, people attending the meetings became more positive about life. They had a clearer sense of purpose and direction in their lives as a result of coming to realize that they were created by a living God. Their lives had a worthwhile purpose. As they developed a relationship with Christ, they sensed freedom from guilt and forgiveness of sin. Acknowledging Jesus as their Lord and receiving His power, they were able to overcome tobacco and alcohol and to be more tolerant of people around them. The Sociology Department of Moscow University was amazed at the practical results of Christianity and at the power of the gospel to change people's lives.

This, of course, was not a surprise to us. We expected it. The Bible makes it plain that when men and women come to Christ, their lives are new and transformed. Christianity is not merely a philosophy or ideology, like Marxism or Communism. Christianity is a living, vital force that transforms the life, because Jesus Himself is alive.

The Apostle Paul makes this point plain in 2 Corinthians 5:17 when he says that if any man is in Christ, old things are passed away and all things are become new. Life is new in Jesus. Christ enshrined in the heart by His Holy Spirit makes a significant difference.

John said in chapter 1 and verse 12 of his Gospel that "As many as received Him [Christ], to them gave He power to become the sons of God."

Receiving Christ is receiving power. Accepting Christ is accepting a new force in the life. Darwin was wrong when he said that human beings are merely biological animals—products of heredity and environment—influences over which we have little or no control.

The gospel says yes, we are influenced by heredity. Certainly we are influenced by our environment. But there is a power stronger than heredity and environment, and that is the power of Jesus Christ. Accepting Christ, we are transformed. Accepting Christ, we are changed. Accepting Christ, a spiritual revolution takes place in the life.

I have seen this spiritual transformation take place in the lives of thousands of people. In our recent meetings in Moscow, over 3,200 people, more than on the day of Pentecost, made decisions for baptism—every one of them a miracle of God's grace, every one of them a testimony to the power of God.

Take Luba, for example. Luba had no interest in the Bible. She had little interest in the things of God. One night she was awakened by a demonic figure standing before her. This evil power enshrouded her in darkness and led her into deep depression. When this power reached out and touched her body, she experienced severe pain in her back.

Luba couldn't sleep all night. Early in the morning, she decided to visit a friend—a friend she believed to be a godly old woman. Luba said, "I need help. I'm in total pain, and I believe I've had an encounter with the devil."

The older woman quietly prayed for Luba. And then she said, "Luba, I'm impressed to tell you something. Seek spiritual guidance from God. Find a teacher—somebody with whom you can study the Bible to learn God's plan for you. In the Bible, you'll meet Christ, and His power will transform your life and deliver you from the evil one. But look for a spiritual teacher to come."

"Where can I find this teacher?" Luba wondered. "How can I ever learn God's plan for my life from His Holy Word, the Bible?" Luba was walking down the streets of Moscow, wondering which way to turn, when she saw a banner for our meetings. She had heard about the meetings on television and read about them in the newspaper. She was impressed that at the Kremlin auditorium she could find spiritual truth—and also find there a teacher to reveal to her the Word of God. To her utter amazement, as she attended the meetings, she discovered the possibility of receiving a Bible and studying a Bible course.

A few days later when I preached on Christ, Luba raised her hand, accepting Jesus. A new peace flooded into her life—a new joy flooded into her soul. And she was a witness to the miraculous transforming power of God's grace. Luba has been baptized. And today she reaches out, influencing her friends for Christ.

One evening after one of the evangelistic meetings, I invited those who wanted to look forward to Bible baptism to come and chat with any one of our staff. After the meeting, Pastor Daniel Ribond from Estonia came to me, bubbling over with excitement. I enthusiastically inquired, "Daniel, what excites you so much tonight?"

"Mark," he answered, "let me share with you an experience I had. After your announcement inviting people forward who were considering baptism, a dignified man in his early sixties came to me. He gave me his business card."

As Daniel handed me the card, my heart leapt for joy. He was the director of the Institute for the Propagation of Science in the Soviet Union—a Ph.D. in philosophy who had spent years of his life teaching Marx and Engles to military officers in the Soviet Army. This man told Pastor Ribond that with the changes in the Soviet Union and with the truth revealed as the Soviet archives were opened, the whole foundation of his life crumbled and fell apart.

"I've no certainty in my life," he told Pastor Ribond. "I have nothing solid to put my feet on—nothing solid to believe in. This has led me back to searching for my roots."

He paused and looked at Pastor Ribond before continuing.

"I want to tell you that my father was a Seventh-day Adventist minister fifty years ago in Moscow. But I left it all for godless atheism. And when I heard the ads for the meetings in the Kremlin, I said, 'I will go.' As I attended, my heart was touched. I could see that here was something to believe in. Here was something with substance. The biblical message of Christ and His soon return provided hope for my troubled, worried heart. I have accepted Jesus and the Bible message. And Pastor, I want to be baptized."

What a miracle! A former teacher of Lenin, Marx, and Engles, converted to the claims of the living Christ! Truly the gods of atheistic Communism are dead, while the Lord of salvation lives. God worked miracle after miracle in Russia. People from all levels of society attended our meetings. People like Ena.

Ena's is another story of a changed life. Hers is the story of the miraculous working of God's power. Ena was born into a well-to-do Moscow family. She ultimately married the son of one of Moscow's mayors. Her husband catapulted himself into a place of prominence in Soviet society. He was in charge of the foreign news service for English broadcasting from Moscow.

Ena herself worked for the very esteemed Progress Publishers for twenty years. For many years she had the responsibility for taking the speeches of Khrushchev, Brezhnev, Andropov, and Gorbachev and comparing the Russian text of those speeches with the English text to make sure that the English was accurate. She had to be certain that there was no better English word to reflect the Russian.

When, in 1988, Mikhail Gorbachev brought together twenty leading thinkers to write a book on perestroika called *No Alternative*, Ena was one of three editors chosen to communicate the message of perestroika to the English-speaking world. She is knowledgeable in philosophy, psychology, and

Pastor and Mrs. Finley and their children with Ena—former editor for Mikhail Gorbachev and other government leaders.

languages. Yet something was missing in her life.

When her husband died, she felt hopelessly alone. She needed comfort and guidance and the warmth of Christ's love filling her heart. One morning she was listening to the radio station called Moscow Echo—the most democratic station in all of Moscow—and she heard an ad for our evangelistic meetings. She came initially to improve her English. But as she attended, the truth of the Word of God touched her heart, and she fell in love with the Christ of God's Word. His relentless, indescribable, incredible love warmed her heart and transformed her life, and she was led to the foot of the cross. There she found freedom from guilt, peace, forgiveness, and a new life in Jesus.

Not long ago I sat down in Ena's home for a lovely meal of borscht and other Russian dishes. Ena looked up at me and said, "Now I am not translating for the leaders of the Soviet Union anymore. But I am translating for the King of Kings, Jesus Christ. My passion now is to make the book called *The Great Controversy* available in the Russian language for my people. I have translated eleven chapters so far. I'm not interested in politics. I'm not interested in psychology. I'm not interested in philosophy. I'm not interested in science. I'm interested in only one thing. My heart hungers after just one thing, and that is to know God's Word—to understand it and to communicate the wonderful principles of Jesus to all those around me."

Christianity is not a form. It is not a ritual. Christianity is not merely a set of beliefs. It's not simply a creed. Christianity has to do with Jesus—the all-loving, all-powerful, transforming Christ. The Christ who can reach into every life and work miracles to change it.

Jesus is real. He reaches out to you. You can come to Him just as Luba, as Anatoli, or as Ena did. And you too can find in Jesus the power for a changed life.

CHAPTER SIX

STANDING AGAINST THE TIDE

Over the centuries, God has always had faithful Christians willing to stand for—and if necessary to die for—His truth. To them, truth was more precious than life itself. Faithfulness to God—and death before dishonor—were their mottos.

These were not spineless, easy-going, accommodating Christians. Their faith was solidly based upon God's Word. Their commitment to Christ meant everything to them—He was the center of their lives. They also understood that compromising their conscience and betraying their religious convictions would bring dishonor to God and would inhibit the forward march of truth.

On December 27, 1503, three of these faithful followers of Christ were burned publicly in wooden cages in Moscow's public square. The most eminent of them, Kuritzyan, the Secretary of State, had begun secretly studying the Bible within the walls of the Kremlin. And the more he studied, the more convinced he became that the Sabbath of the fourth commandment was to be faithfully kept by Christians today. He read these words in John 14:15: "If you love Me, keep My commandments." And Kuritzyan became convinced that love for Christ led to obedience.

As he studied the Genesis account of creation in Genesis 2:1-3, he read: "Thus the heavens and the earth were finished and all the host of them. And on the seventh day God ended His work which He had made and He rested on the seventh day from all His work which He had made. And God blessed the seventh day and sanctified it because that in it He had rested from all His work which God created and made."

Kuritzyan reasoned that if God had set the Sabbath aside at creation, it had been established over 2,300 years before the existence of the Jewish nation—meaning that 119,000 Sabbaths were kept before the Jews existed as a people. Therefore, the Sabbath could not be an exclusively Jewish institution, since God had given it to the entire human race.

When he read the Ten Commandments, he noted the fourth commandment, which said: "Remember the Sabbath day to keep it holy. Six days shalt thou labor and do all thy work, but the seventh day is the Sabbath of the Lord thy God. In it thou shalt not do any work. Thou nor thy son nor thy daughter nor thy manservant nor thy cattle nor the stranger that is within thy gates. For in six days the Lord made heaven and earth, the sea and all that in them is."

Kuritzyan clearly saw that the Sabbath had been written with God's own finger on tables of stone, never to be eradicated, never to be erased. He shared the Sabbath truth with Ivan Maximo and Tasia the Arch Immandrite of the Jury Monastery of Novogrote. Each of these two friends accepted the truth of the Sabbath.

When the Czar and the church leaders learned that these three had become faithful, Sabbath-keeping Christians, they were enraged. Their fury led them to put the three men into wooden cages in what today is Moscow's Red Square. They were pelted with tomatoes and eggs and then publicly burned on December 27, 1503.

The Czar militantly attempted to destroy their convictions regarding the Sabbath truth. It is possible to kill people, but you can never kill the truth. And one day those who have believed in truth and lived for truth will arise from dusty graves to ascend to heaven, there to be loyal to Christ forever. Over the centuries, faithful Sabbath-keeping Christians in Russia have paid with their lives for believing the truth of God's Word.

In 1929 Stalin decided to attempt to eradicate Christianity in Russia. Legislation was enacted that bound the church hand and foot. Anatoli Steponovich, a dear friend of mine in Moscow, told me that one day when he went to choir practice in the Moscow church, KGB officers broke in and took the pastor and every elder and deacon to prison. Anatoli suffered terribly for six years in prison. But during that six-year period he was faithful to Christ and did not yield his conscientious convictions. He was able—even in prison—to keep faithfully the Bible Sabbath.

No doubt one of the more thrilling stories of faith to emerge from the former Soviet Union is that of Division President Mikhail Kulakov. One day years ago, an woman approached Pastor Kulakov indicating a spiritual interest. As a friendship developed between the two of them, Pastor Kulakov began studying the Bible with her. She asked question after question regarding the Bible. Pastor Kulakov, of course, was delighted to answer her spiritual questions from the Bible.

After a few meetings, he was suddenly arrested by the KGB and charged with the crime of spreading anti-state propaganda. The individual with whom he had been studying claimed that he was being pressured into accepting Christianity. The whole thing had been a setup.

Pastor Kulakov received a life sentence to be spent in exile and was sent thousands of miles away to Central Asia to spend the rest of his life. Faithfulness to Christ led to the loss of all his dreams. But our God is greater than any adverse circumstances. Our God is a big God—far bigger than any of our trials. As the Apostle Paul triumphantly declared, "We know that all things work together for good to those who love God." Romans 8:28.

During his exile, Pastor Kulakov met the woman God designed to be his wife. And miraculously, at the end of only six years he was allowed to return home, bringing with him his new bride. As He did for Jacob in a foreign land, God worked for the good of Pastor Kulakov.

In recent years others have also suffered insults and humiliation for their faith. I met Aleksey during our evangelistic meetings in the Kremlin Hall in Moscow. In 1989, Aleksey first accepted Jesus Christ. As a senior economist in the Department of Foreign Affairs, he suffered intensely for making a commitment to Jesus.

"I started finding my way to Jesus in 1989 by beginning to read the Bible," he recalled. "I tried to find myself a shelter from the cruel world that surrounded me. I became interested in the gospel, but unfortunately, I soon had personal evidence of the persecution, humiliation, and insult that would come to me for my religious convictions.

"I then made a mistake. I told some of my friends at my work in government about my visits to church. I wanted to interest them in the gospel, but they only spread the news of my religious interest. As a result, I was expelled from Komsomol [the Communist youth organization]. Only my personal acquaintance with the leader of Komsomol's head organization in Moscow helped me hush up a great scandal—

that someone in a position of responsibility in the Communist structure should become a Christian.

"I became the subject of discrimination at my job. I worked as the senior economist in the Department of Foreign Affairs. But beginning in 1988, I became interested in personal computers. A few months before the scandal over my conversion, I had managed to convince my chief to send me away to study programming, and the firm paid for the first year of the training. I worked and studied in the evenings. But when the next year came, the administration refused to pay for a second year, so I couldn't complete my education.

"Nonetheless, I had a strong desire to study, so I continued with self-education. I created a network based on applications for automation of the financial and accounting departments. I worked hard day and night because I am enthusiastic and energetic by nature, but I received only humiliation and insults because I'd become a Christian.

"Now that I've accepted the seventh-day Bible Sabbath, I still face the same humiliations and insults. Yet my heart is filled with the peace of God."

Misunderstanding and religious intolerance still exists on the part of some in the Soviet Union. Old prejudices against truth remain, yet God has faithful men and women of character who are willing to stand for the truth though the heavens fall. God has faithful men and women of integrity who have made a decision to live for Christ no matter what happens around them.

Ellen White stated it so succinctly when she said on page 57 of the book *Education*:

> The greatest want of the world is the want of men . . . men whose conscience is as true to duty as the needle to the pole, men who will stand for the right though the heavens fall.

When the final history of the world is written in God's record book—when the secrets of the ages are made plain—it will be seen that multitudes of men and women in Russia have been faithful to Christ over the centuries. They have suffered imprisonment. They have suffered persecution. And they have suffered death. Yet they will be the honored of Christ in heaven. Their prayers, their suffering, and their tears have opened up miraculous doors for the proclamation of the truth. God has faithfully answered their prayers.

CHAPTER SEVEN

LENIN'S LINES ARE GONE

After one of the evangelistic meetings, a reporter from a leading Moscow newspaper asked for an interview. Our meetings had been featured on the evening news on most of the Moscow channels for the entire week. Newspaper coverage was widespread as well. Thousands continued to attend our meetings.

Yet this interview was different than any I had ever experienced before. The reporter began by asking the question, "Have you visited Lenin's tomb?"

"Yes," I replied, "I have—why do you ask?"

Lenin's tomb is an imposing structure located in the center of Red Square. Lines to get into that tomb used to be five or six hours long. Today, however, except for a few tourists who may delay you ten or fifteen minutes, entering the tomb is quite simple.

I was awestruck as I walked into the tomb, down the steps, through the black granite passageways, and then into the

Pastor Finley received special permission to photograph and film Lenin's tomb. The lord of socialism is dead—but the Lord of our salvation is alive!

large open chamber where the embalmed body of Lenin lay on a covered bed-like pedestal encased in glass. Scores in front of me walked by in reverential awe as they looked at Lenin.

I was impressed by the simple fact that Lenin is dead. He no longer continues to rule the nation, influencing millions with his political philosophy.

The reporter sitting before me rapidly fired off his questions.

"Mr. Finley, what is your impression of Lenin? Was he a good man—or a bad man? But most of all, Mr. Finley, I want to ask you, where is Lenin now? Is he in heaven—or is he in hell? Give me a straightforward answer."

How thankful I was to know the truth about the state of the dead. New Age spiritualism permeates Russia. Atheism left a spiritual vacuum. Millions have become involved with spiritualism. In the survey mentioned earlier, taken by Moscow University, researchers discovered that a misunderstanding of death was deeply imbedded in the Russian mind. Therefore, I was encouraged to share what the Bible really teaches about death.

I then shared with him Ecclesiastes 9:5, which says, "The living know that they shall die, but the dead know not anything." "Sir," I commented, "death is an unconscious sleep. Those who die wait for the final resurrection and judgment."

We then read what Jesus Himself had declared in John 5:29: "And [they] shall come forth; they that have done good unto the resurrection of life, and they that have done evil unto the resurrection of damnation."

As we continued our Bible study about death, we discussed the story of Lazarus.

Speaking about the death of His friend Lazarus, Jesus said in John 11:11-14: "Our friend Lazarus is sleeping." Then He declared, "I go that I may wake him out of sleep." When Christ called Lazarus from the tomb and said, "Lazarus, come forth," Lazarus rose from sleep. Jesus didn't say, "Lazarus, come down."

Lazarus did not spend four days in heaven enjoying its bliss, after which Christ demanded that he return. That would have shown a grievous lack of consideration and would also have been the height of insult. Lazarus was sleeping when he was resurrected.

In fact, Martha, who learned her faith directly from Jesus, spoke of her resurrection hope in these words: "Master, I know that my brother shall rise again in the last day." John 11:24. Martha believed there would be a resurrection at the last day and that she would see her brother then. As a testimony that Christ could raise the dead on the last day, He raised Lazarus from the dead.

The Apostle Paul makes the state of the dead abundantly plain when he says in 1 Thessalonians 4:16, 17: "The Lord Himself shall descend from heaven with a shout, with the voice of the archangel, and with the trump of God, and the dead in Christ shall rise first. Then we which are alive and remain shall be caught up to meet them and be with the Lord forever."

The Bible makes it clear that death is a sleep until the resurrection.

"So," I concluded to my interviewer, "Lenin is neither in heaven nor in hell—he is sleeping as he awaits the final judgment."

He then asked a second question.

"Yes, from your answer I understand that. But how will Lenin fare in the final judgment? Will he be saved or lost? And how is a person saved?"

What an opportunity! Recognizing that his questions went much deeper than simply the fate of Lenin, my goal was to interest him in the gospel. I quoted Acts 16:30, where the Philippian jailer had asked, "Sir, what must I do to be saved?"

And then I shared the Apostle Paul's response: "Believe on the Lord Jesus Christ and thou shalt be saved."

I pointed out that there were many good leaders in the world, and also some bad leaders. But none of them could provide hope for eternal life. Lenin was still in his tomb, but Jesus Christ has burst the bonds of the tomb. Christ claimed to be the Son of God. He claimed to be divine. He claimed to have come down from heaven. He claimed to be able to offer us eternal life.

And He says, "Believe on Me. Believe that I am the Son of God. Believe that I died to forgive your sins. Believe that I died to free you from guilt. Believe that I can transform your life—and believe that I can resurrect you from the grave."

So leaders may be good or they may be bad, but only Christ is eternal. And only Christ can enable us to live forever.

"We need one whose tomb is not filled, Sir, as Lenin's tomb is," I told the reporter. "We need one whose tomb is empty. And that's the tomb of Christ."

Not yet fully content with my answers, he responded, "I still have another question. In the final judgment, do you think Lenin will be judged as a good man—or a bad man?"

"Sir," I replied, "Lenin did a number of good things. He had many noble and praiseworthy ideas, but I believe that in the light of God's judgment, any man who clings to an atheistic, anti-God philosophy will be found lacking in God's sight. I also believe that the life of such a man would ultimately be judged both by his own nation and by history itself to be negative rather than positive. It seems to me that what this country needs is not only the philosophy of Lenin, but the power of Jesus Christ to transform and change lives."

The reporter thanked me for the interview and said, "Look for an article in the paper. It will be published soon."

With eager anticipation we continued to watch the papers for the next few days. Soon the article we were waiting for appeared. The front page of the paper had a bold headline that read something like this: "WHERE IS LENIN NOW? ONLY MARK FINLEY KNOWS. TURN TO PAGE SIX." And there on page six was a complete article with all the Bible texts we had given the reporter. There in the newspaper was a complete study from the Bible on how to be saved through Jesus Christ.

We believe God used that reporter's questions to communicate truth to millions. They once lined up at Lenin's tomb, but they're not lining up there anymore. They're lining up today to get Bibles. They're lining up today to purchase tickets for our evangelistic meetings. They're lining up today to learn to know and to study God's Word.

Let me tell you about a Soviet military officer—a man named Alex. In an interview, I asked him, "Alex, what were you doing a year ago?"

"I was a Soviet military officer," he responded. "I was teaching my fellow officers atheistic, godless materialism."

"And what's your life like today, Alex," I continued. "How has it changed?"

"My life before had no foundation," he replied. "It was filled with confusion. My existence was totally depressing. I really had no purpose for my life. But now I have set Christ as my foundation. I have found Jesus as my Savior. He is my solid hope for the future."

To see the smile on that officer's face—to see the joy in his eyes and to sense his commitment to Christ—was a wonderful thrill. He has been baptized as a Seventh-day Adventist Christian and serves as a deacon in our new church in the Plahanov Hall. He was in charge of the food distribution program we conducted in Moscow, in which over twenty tons of food were distributed to needy families.

The hunger of the Russian people, though, is not merely for physical food, but for the Bread of Life. In 1991, over

4,000 people attended our evangelistic meetings in the Plahanov Hall. Amazingly enough, they completed 77,000 Bible lessons in just three weeks! At the conclusion of the meetings, we baptized over 600 people.

In our recent 1992 Kremlin meetings, we initially reserved 12,000 Bibles. But after only two nights, we ran out. We then purchased 4,000 more, distributed those, and again ran out. Ultimately we distributed over 20,000 Bibles. Our attendees completed more than 250,000 Bible lessons!

Pastor Don Gray and his wife, Marge, coordinated a Bible study program for our meetings. Combining the totals from meetings in the summer of 1991 and spring of 1992, nearly 25,000 Bibles were distributed, with participants completing over 350,000 Bible lessons.

It is absolutely incredible to see the changes that happen in people's lives as the result of studying and knowing God's Word. It reminds me of David's statement in Psalms: "My heart panteth after thee, O God, as the deer pants after the water brooks."

After seventy years of atheistic oppression—seventy years of Communism and religious persecution—the hearts of men and women are open today to study God's Word.

Over 100 pastors spent hours during the meetings correcting Bible lessons.

A high-ranking military officer came to our meetings. He works in the area of strategic defense and is an engineer who designs weapon systems for his country. In a private interview he said to me, "Pastor, I really want to be baptized. I've accepted Jesus Christ. I've accepted the principles and truths of the Bible. But I have to take orders from the high command on strategic defense. I design very sophisticated secret weapon systems. Is it possible for me to be a faithful Christian if I have to take orders from strategic command? I really need your counsel. What do you think?" We spent over an hour talking about the kingdom of God and discussing what it means to be a radical disciple for Christ. I pointed out to him that he is now a member of a new kingdom and has an even higher position. He's now an ambassador for Jesus Christ.

"Does this mean the end of my military career?" he asked.

I pointed out that I couldn't make that decision for him—that he'd have to make it. I quoted John 8:29, where Jesus said, "I do always those things that please Him."

Here is a fundamental principle in life: When we seek

Christ and His kingdom first, He will work out the problems of our life. That military officer and I knelt and sought God together. We prayed together.

"Lord," he prayed, "whatever You want me to do—even if it means my job and my career—I want to do. I'm giving my life to You, Lord. I'm asking You for help and direction and guidance for my future."

What courage! What faith! No, my friends, they are not lining up for Lenin's tomb anymore! Even military officers are following a new leader—not Lenin, but Jesus Christ.

We stayed in the same hotel as the deputies from the Russian Parliament. For most of April, 1992, these deputies were participating in parliamentary proceedings within the Kremlin. Our Adventist pastors stayed in the Russia Hotel for the first two weeks of April as well. When the deputies moved in, our pastors had to move out.

As often happens, the hotels in Moscow were filled, and the pastors had no place to move. This meant that fifty pastors and seminary students had to leave the Russia Hotel with no place to stay.

The president of the Russian Union, Pastor Murga, along with the local conference president, Pastor Trichor, began looking for another place to house the pastors. They made contact with the Salute Hotel. As they discussed their housing needs with the manager and identified themselves as Seventh-day Adventists working in the Kremlin evangelistic meetings, his eyes brightened.

"This is very interesting," he said. "One of the owners of our hotel has been attending your meetings. She told me about them. I want you to meet her."

He invited our pastors to sit and wait while he contacted the owner. Upon meeting them, she asked, "Are you with the Kremlin crusade and the evangelistic meetings being held there now on the Bible?"

They responded positively.

"Your pastors must be hungry," she continued. "Are they waiting in the bus? I'll open up my restaurant right now. Supper is on me."

The entire group then ate supper on the house.

"I am so impressed with your work," the owner told them. "And I'm going to give you an entire floor in my hotel. I appreciate these meetings. I want to do something special."

Our pastors were given the entire floor of the hotel at a very reduced rate. Imagine having a whole hotel full of Seventh-day Adventist pastors! Each evening after the owner returned from the meetings, she discussed what she had heard with the pastors. They stayed up late into the night discussing the Bible, Christ, and the things of eternity. Often during the evening, she'd open her restaurant and feed them for free.

As she continued attending the meetings, she said, "I have now found direction for my life. This is precious to me. Here is something I can have as a foundation under my feet. Here is something solid and secure that will not fade as time goes by. I want to be baptized as an Adventist Christian."

Our great problem today in Moscow is churches. The lines are much shorter to Lenin's tomb, but the lines to our churches are getting longer. One year ago we had 900 members in Moscow; today we have 3,000 members. Yet we have no church buildings. Three other groups are meeting in rented public facilities.

Our church at the Plahanov Hall now has 1,200 members. We started two other churches after this Kremlin crusade—one in a place called Azlik, with 500 members, and another in a place called ZVI, also with 500 members.

After the hotel owner attended our evangelistic meetings and was baptized, she joyfully exclaimed, "My great desire is to build a church in this city for the honor and glory of Christ."

As our evangelistic series in the Kremlin came to an end

Plahanov Hall—the site of one of our new churches, with a current membership of 1,200.

with over 3,200 people making decisions for baptism, hundreds more attended our baptismal classes. I met together with our staff—Don Gray, our campaign manager; and Dan

Over 3,200 people made decisions for baptism. Over 1,300 have already been baptized as this book is first published.

Benzinger, my associate evangelist—and discussed with them what we were going to do for one final baptism.

We desired to start three new churches in the city and looked forward to a final baptism in which we would bus in 8- to 10 thousand people as spectators and baptize between 1,000 and 1,500 people. We believed that this would be one of the most significant experiences in the life of the church in Moscow.

We began looking for baptismal sites. One of the sites that attracted us very much was an outdoor swimming pool—really a miniature lake. It was here in 1932 that Stalin blew up one of the most beautiful Orthodox cathedrals in Moscow to put an end to Christianity. We thought, what if we could hold a baptism at this site? It would be a symbol that Christianity was being launched in Russia again.

After meeting with the management of the pool, the director seemed quite enthusiastic initially. It appeared there would be no difficulty with our holding the baptism. But at a second meeting, he seemed much more hesitant. About halfway through the conversation he looked up at me and said," Mr. Finley, if you baptize that many people here, it could cause difficulty. Some religious leaders consider this to be a very holy site. It's very likely that they could react negatively—even with physical violence—at your meeting. I'm not prepared to take that risk unless the city authorities pass an ordinance permitting the baptism and providing a police contingent to protect both the spectators and those being baptized."

From the look of concern on his face, I immediately recognized that it wouldn't be wise to proceed with the baptism at the Moscow swimming pool location. Only one other place in town that I knew of would house the thousands that might come to the baptism. We had already explored the Olympic swimming pool as a site, but had encountered logistical problems with the necessity of lowering the water level. The pool is over six feet deep—too deep for a baptism unless the water was lowered—and the pool has a complicated filtration system that a baptism would necessitate shutting down for ten to twelve days.

We attempted to rent another pool in a sports training facility south of Moscow. We spent three or four hours in preliminary meetings with the general manager of the pool. Then, in a final two-hour meeting, we agreed on a price and were preparing to sign a contract for the use of the pool. As we finalized on details, we checked out the speaker system, looked at the dressing rooms for men and women, and had everything arranged.

Two minutes before we were to leave the general director's office, his telephone rang. The voice on the other end of the line belonged to his superior, who emphatically stated, "You must cancel all plans for a baptism at our complex. You're forbidden to rent the pool for the baptism. Any preliminary negotiations you've made are finished."

The director of the pool hung up the phone. His hands were shaking, and his countenance had changed dramatically. He looked at me nervously and said, "I can't explain this—I don't understand the reason for it, but you cannot use the pool. I can't rent it to you. I've been forbidden to do that."

"Can you at least explain why?" I asked.

"There is no good reason that I know of," he answered.

We had no choice but to shake hands and leave. As I got into the car that day, I thought of Paul's statement in 1 Corinthians 16:9: "For a great door and effectual is opened unto me, but there are many adversaries."

"God," I prayed, "You have worked so powerfully. You have moved so dramatically, Lord. You have opened hearts. Thousands have come to the meetings and made decisions for baptism. They have completed the Bible course. Our pastors have been interviewing them individually. They've gone through the baptismal class. But we have no place to baptize them."

We became convinced that unseen forces were at work attempting to inhibit the work of God. Could there be fanatical religious leaders putting pressure on these directors? Were hard-line Communists still opposing our work? We didn't know! One thing we did know is that unseen forces were at work attempting to hinder the work of God.

Discussing it as a staff, we determined that we would not mention over the telephone any sites being considered for our baptisms. We would dramatically change our strategy. Rather than one mass baptism, we would attempt to rent smaller halls and smaller pools.

We planned baptisms for a Wednesday night, a Thursday night, and a Sabbath afternoon. We baptized people in smaller groups of three to four hundred in these smaller halls. We desired to attract far less public attention.

Evidence that the Holy Spirit had led in our decision to conduct baptisms in several less-publicized locations surfaced on April 14—a few days after our first major baptism. One of Moscow's newspapers ran a story with a headline something like this: "NOT THE JORDAN RIVER OR A HOLY ORTHODOX CATHEDRAL, BUT AN ORDINARY SWIMMING POOL." The article proceeded to argue that it is sinful to be baptized in such a common location as a swimming pool.

It was now unmistakably obvious that forces were at work to discourage people from making decisions for Christ. In my next news interview, one of the first questions asked was, "Is it wrong to baptize people in a swimming pool?"

"It is not the location that is holy," I responded. "During the years of atheistic Communism, people were baptized in large rain barrels, in mud holes, in drainage ditches, in bathtubs, and in any conceivable place where there was enough water to be immersed.

"It is not holy water—but the grace of Jesus Christ—that

saves us. Baptism by immersion expresses biblical faith. It is a public statement of belief in Christ—the public declaration of a desire to follow Him."

When it came time for the baptisms, the negative press did nothing to discourage the converted candidates or to interfere with the baptismal service. Hundreds walked into the baptismal pools to follow their Lord and Savior, Jesus Christ. Forty-five buses transported candidates to three separate baptisms.

At our first baptism, it took fourteen buses to bring the candidates. Eleven buses were required to transport candidates and friends to the second baptism, and twenty buses were needed for the third.

The lines at Lenin's tomb are shorter and shorter. But people are lining up to come to evangelistic meetings. They are lining up to get Bibles. They are lining up to attend church. And they are lining up to board buses to baptismal sites.

At each baptism, the halls were packed with eager baptismal candidates. So many were being baptized they could hardly find standing room around the swimming pools. Twenty-two pastors entered the water at one baptism and baptized their candidates in the name of the Father, and the Son, and the Holy Spirit.

Truly the message of Christ is going forward. Truly the stronghold of atheism is being penetrated with the gospel. From what we have seen, the teachings of Jesus are outstripping the teachings of Marx. Truly Revelation 14:6, 7 is being fulfilled: "And I saw another angel fly in the midst of heaven, having the everlasting gospel to preach unto them that dwell on the earth, and to every nation, and kindred, and tongue, and people."

An angel flying in mid-heaven. God's last day message—the message of the uplifted Christ. The message of the life-changing Christ. The message of the all-powerful Christ. The message of His love and law. The message of His Word and truth. The message of His urgent return in glory and in splendor. This is the message going to the world.

Before our eyes, with the dissolution of the Soviet Union and the opening of doors for the proclamation of the gospel, we are witnessing the fulfillment of prophecy. Christ is reaching out and touching and changing lives in the former Soviet Union.

One of the greatest examples of His ability to change lives and to transform men and women from within occurred during our baptismal service on Wednesday night, April 15.

Often while in Moscow, we passed what I called KGB corner. Three huge KGB buildings, housing thousands of KGB officers, dominated the corner. Here too was the famous KGB Leubianka Prison. In the center of the traffic circle in front of the KGB complex stood the statue of Feliks Dzerzhinsky, founder of the KGB. Shortly after the failure of the August 1991 coup, Moscow workmen and residents, seething with frustration, drove a crane into the center of the traffic circle and dismounted the statue. They left it dangling for days from a steel-cable noose, high above the street.

What a shocking symbol of the triumph of democratic freedom over totalitarian fear! Photographs of that hanging statue of the KGB founder appeared on the front page of news journals such as *Time* and *Newsweek* and newspapers throughout the world.

But there is an untold story of love and faith and of the triumph of the gospel behind it all. The grandson of one of the early leaders of the KGB accepted Christ and Bible truth and became a Seventh-day Adventist. He has been one of my translators during my last two evangelistic campaigns in Moscow. At our baptism on April 15, where over 350 were baptized, he was translating for me as we joyously watched twenty pastors enter the water and baptize candidate after candidate.

Finally, in the midst of that great throng being baptized, a Jewish poetess entered the water. Leonid, my translator and grandson of an early KGB leader, had studied the Bible some with the poetess Tatyanya. As she was baptized and came up out of the water soaking wet, he was so overcome with emotion that he said, "Mark, I can no longer translate for you. I must go and greet her. I must go and express my thanksgiving to God for her baptism."

So I stood alone as Leonid walked over to Tatyanya. He put his arms around her, and in Christian kindness and love and dignity, expressed his joy in Jesus in her baptism.

I thought to myself, Where else could this take place? What other power could accomplish this? The grandson of this KGB leader—the same KGB that had so ruthlessly persecuted and destroyed millions of Jews—embracing a Jewish poetess in Christian love!

My mind then flashed to another scene. On the pedestal of the statue of Feliks Dzerzhinsky, a wooden cross has been mounted today. Throughout the former Soviet Union, the cross of Christ, the gospel of Christ, the love of Christ, and the power of Christ have triumphed. Throughout Moscow today are powerful symbols of Christ's triumph.

One of the Kremlin's gates is called "The Savior's Gate." Truly, thousands entered through the gates of the Kremlin to meet their Savior in the spring of 1992. The cross has triumphed.

On each corner of the Kremlin towers is a huge red star weighing between a ton and a ton and a half. Viewing the Kremlin from a distance, the dominant impression is not of the red stars on the Kremlin towers, but of the many magnificent cathedrals. Each dome shines brilliantly in the Moscow sunlight.

THE CROSS AND THE KREMLIN

There above the Kremlin, even after seventy years of godless atheism, scores of crosses stand atop elegant golden-domed cathedrals, speaking of the ultimate triumph of the crucified, resurrected, and soon-coming Christ. These magnificent crosses are a powerful, silent testimony that Jesus Christ is alive in the hearts of His people.

After decades of Communism, the cross still stands over the Kremlin! ❑

THE HARVEST

Hundreds gather on the banks of a beautiful Moscow lake in July of 1991 for the first outdoor mass baptism in the city in 40 years.

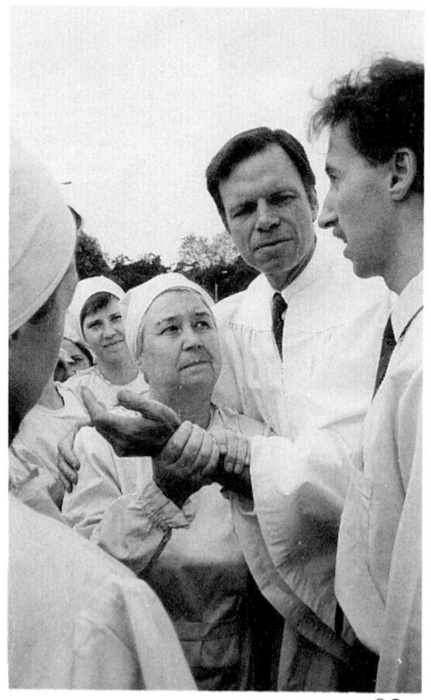

Pastor Finley and his translator instruct a happy baptismal candidate.

The Russians love flowers. They symbolize the new life of these baptismal candidates.

With flowers and a smile, Mark and Ernestine Finley warmly welcome the newly baptized candidates into the family of God.

In the last year, over 2,000 people have been baptized in Moscow.

Filled with Christ's joy, hundreds were baptized in the spring of 1992.

"And this gospel of the kingdom shall be preached in all the world for a witness unto all nations; and then shall the end come . . . . Go ye therefore, and teach all nations, baptizing them in the name of the Father, and of the Son, and of the Holy Ghost" (Matthew 24:14; 28:19).